Praise fo

In a fast-changing culture th... as Christians seem alien to many in the culture!), it is easy for Christians to throw up their hands in despair and adopt a purely defensive mode. In this important book, Tim Keller unpacks the gospel and gently but firmly reminds us that it is nonnegotiable. At the same time, he enables us to think through how we can responsibly interact with the culture, how we can — indeed, must — appreciate good things within it, and how we can firmly and faithfully apply the gospel to it. But this is not a mechanical how-to book; rather, it is a reflective meditation on some hugely important themes in Scripture written by someone who has exercised faithful pastoral ministry in a major city for two decades.

> D. A. CARSON, research professor of
> New Testament, Trinity Evangelical Divinity School

No one has listened more closely to the harmonies of city, culture, church, and Scripture than Tim Keller. In *Center Church*, he not only describes the different strains of music but also tells us how he has orchestrated the results for the sake of ministry outreach and renewal. Now it's our turn to listen, as Tim practically yet powerfully prepares us to participate in this great symphony of the gospel.

> BRYAN CHAPELL, president, Covenant Theological Seminary

Center Church is an immensely helpful resource for the next generation of church leaders. It is theologically profound, thought provoking, and energizing, and it will make you uncomfortable in measure. Once again, Tim Keller has hit the bull's-eye!

> ALISTAIR BEGG, senior pastor,
> Parkside Church, Cleveland, Ohio

We don't need another "do ministry like my church does ministry" book. Nor do we need another book that critiques other church models. We need a book that helps us think critically and biblically as we structure our churches. *Center Church* is packed with Tim Keller's experience, humility, and wisdom. This book will help you if you are serious about seeing your city transformed by the gospel of grace.

DARRIN PATRICK, lead pastor,
The Journey, St. Louis, Missouri

Church leaders abandon their unique calling if they merely think theologically to the exclusion of seeing the world in light of the gospel and helping their churches live in the world with gospel wisdom. No one makes this case more clearly today than Tim Keller. He resists the all-too-easy pattern of selling a simple model of what it means to be the church that fits every setting. Instead he brings to life the myriad ways churches are called to be faithful and fruitful in their own unique cultural context. Read this book if you want to learn how to ask the really important (and difficult) questions by which the gospel confronts our ecclesial identity.

RICHARD LINTS, Andrew Mutch distinguished professor
of theology, Gordon-Conwell Theological Seminary

Cities are challenging and complex but also important and strategic. And those who are called to minister in cities need encouragement and resources that fuel hope and effectiveness. That's why I'm so glad that Tim Keller has written this book. His passion for the gospel, heart for the city, and vision of a movement of the Holy Spirit that will transform lives and bring hope and peace to our cities has compelled him to share his insights and thinking with us. What's more, the church he serves speaks to the integrity of his heart and the possibility of the reality of this vision. Be prepared. Your thinking will be sharpened, and your heart will be moved.

DR. CRAWFORD W. LORITTS JR., senior pastor,
Fellowship Bible Church, Roswell, Georgia

This outstanding book, like the Manhattan ministry out of which it has come, shows how Reformed theological acumen and wise pastoral intelligence may combine to achieve spiritual fruitfulness in urban contexts everywhere. Every page illuminates. Keller is a huge gift to today's church.

J. I. PACKER, professor emeritus, Regent College

Most of us observe and see the obvious. Tim Keller observes and sees that which is unseen by others—especially when it comes to the truth of God's Word and the culture of the day. Once again, he has given us deeper insights—this time regarding the church and how she can experience her healthiest potential. How foolish to know of this book and not read it!

RANDY POPE, pastor, Perimeter Church, Atlanta, Georgia

Tim Keller has given us the must-read book on gospel-shaped ministry. Robustly theological and profoundly practical, it is a top-to-bottom survey of gospel implications for the life and ministry of the church. The gap between biblical and practical theology is masterfully bridged. Having worked with Tim and Redeemer City to City, I have benefited from the content of this book and can also attest to its profound influence on ministers and churches throughout the world. This is not simply curriculum content; it is exactly the kind of life-giving, generative gospel theology our churches need. No thoughtful Christian's bookshelf should be without it.

STEPHEN T. UM, senior minister,
Citylife Presbyterian Church, Boston, Massachusetts

In *Center Church*, one of the great missionary statesmen of our time lays out a vision of the church vigorous enough to transform entire cities through its agency of the gospel. Tim Keller is a gifted teacher, an outstanding leader, and an exemplary disciple of Jesus. A worthy read!

ALAN HIRSCH, founder of 100Movements and
the Forge Mission Training Network

We live in a day of remarkable church leaders and wonderful Christian thinkers, but I'm not sure there's a more thoughtful church leader in our day than Tim Keller. *Center Church* is his call for church ministry formed by deep theological reflection and sensitive cultural exegesis executed by courageous leaders so that the city may once more flourish under the gospel.

JOHN ORTBERG, senior pastor,
Menlo Park Presbyterian Church, Menlo Park, California

Tim Keller's church in New York City serves as one of the world's best models for gospel-centered ministry that wisely, biblically, and fruitfully connects with its community. This is mainly due to Dr. Keller's deep understanding of the gospel and his exceptional gift for interpreting culture. His latest book will be immensely helpful to anyone doing ministry anywhere. *Center Church* is not a manual for replicating Keller's ministry, but something much more important: a theological vision for how the gospel of Jesus Christ relates to culture, ministry, and the Christian life.

PHILIP RYKEN, president, Wheaton College

I'm not exaggerating when I say that *Center Church* is my favorite book Tim Keller has written thus far. Perhaps this book simply represents the distillation of Tim's wisdom — the synthesis of years of marinating in the gospel, exegeting the text of Scripture, and engaging the soul of our culture; his willingness to dialogue without diatribe; his ongoing commitment to think through the radical implications of God's grace; his great love for Jesus' bride, God's kingdom, and the history of redemption. It's all refreshingly here. What an awesome and practical read! I cannot wait to use this book with emerging leaders and churches willing to dream.

SCOTTY SMITH, founding pastor,
Christ Community Church, Franklin, Tennessee

SHAPED BY THE
GOSPEL

Center Church Series

Shaped by the Gospel
(with new contributions by
Michael Horton and Dane Ortlund)

Loving the City
(with new contributions by
Daniel Strange, Gabriel Salguero,
and Andy Crouch)

Serving a Movement
(with new contributions by
Tim Chester, Daniel Montgomery
and Mike Cosper, and Alan Hirsch)

SHAPED BY THE GOSPEL

DOING BALANCED, GOSPEL-CENTERED MINISTRY IN YOUR CITY

A New Edition of
Section One
of Center Church

TIMOTHY KELLER

WITH NEW CONTRIBUTIONS BY
MICHAEL HORTON AND DANE ORTLUND

ZONDERVAN

Shaped by the Gospel
Copyright © 2016 by Redeemer City to City, Timothy J. Keller, and Zondervan

This title is also available as a Zondervan ebook. Visit www.zondervan.com/ebooks.

Requests for information should be addressed to:

Zondervan, 3900 *Sparks Dr. SE, Grand Rapids, Michigan 49546*

Library of Congress Cataloging-in-Publication Data

Names: Keller, Timothy, 1950- author. | Horton, Michael Scott. | Ortlund, Dane Calvin. |
    Keller, Timothy, 1950- Center church. Contained in (work):
Title: Shaped by the Gospel : doing balanced, Gospel-centered ministry in your city /
    Timothy Keller ; with new contributions by Michael Horton and Dane Ortlund.
Description: Zondervan, Grand Rapids, MI, USA : Zondervan, [2015] | Revised editon of:
    Section 1 of Center church. Grand Rapis, MI : Zondervan, c2012. | "A new edition of
    Section 1." | Includes bibliographical references.
Identifiers: LCCN 2015041228 | ISBN 9780310520597 (softcover)
Subjects: LCSH: City missions. | City churches. | Church work. | Evangelistic work.
Classification: LCC BV2653 .K452 2015 | DDC 253—dc23 LC record available at http://
    lccn.loc.gov/2015041228

Cover design: Lucas Art and Design
Interior design: Kait Lamphere

Printed in the United States of America

---

16 17 18 19 20 21 /DHV/ 20 19 18 17 16 15 14 13 12 11 10 9 8 7 6 5 4 3 2 1

CONTENTS

CONTENTS

SERIES
INTRODUCTION

Two kinds of books are ordinarily written for pastors and church leaders. One kind lays out general biblical principles for all churches. These books start with scriptural exegesis and biblical theology and list the characteristics and functions of a true biblical church. The most important characteristic is that a ministry be faithful to the Word and sound in doctrine, but these books also rightly call for biblical standards of evangelism, church leadership, community and membership, worship, and service.

Another category of book operates at the opposite end of the spectrum. These books do not spend much time laying biblical theological foundations, though virtually all of them cite biblical passages. Instead, they are practical "how-to" books that describe specific mind-sets, programs, and ways to do church. This genre of book exploded onto the scene during the church growth movement of the 1970s and 1980s through the writing of authors such as C. Peter Wagner and Robert Schuller. A second generation of books in a similar vein appeared with personal accounts of successful churches, authored by senior pastors, distilling practical principles for others to use. A third generation of practical church books began more than ten years ago. These are volumes that directly criticize the church growth how-to books. Nevertheless, they also consist largely of case studies and pictures of what a good church looks like on the ground, with practical advice on how to organize and conduct ministry.

From these latter volumes I have almost always profited, coming away from each book with at least one good idea I could use. But by and large, I found the books less helpful than I hoped they would be. Implicitly or explicitly, they made near-absolutes out of techniques and models that had worked in a certain place at a certain time. I was fairly certain that many of these methods would not work in my context in New York and were not as universally applicable as the authors implied. In particular, church leaders outside of the United States found these books irritating because the authors assumed that what worked in a suburb of a U.S. city would work almost anywhere.

As people pressed me to speak and write about our experience at Redeemer, I realized that most were urging me to write my own version of the second type of book. Pastors did not want me to recapitulate biblical doctrine and principles of church life they had gotten in seminary. Instead, they were looking for a "secrets of success" book. They wanted instructions for specific programs and techniques that appealed to urban people. One pastor said, "I've tried the Willow Creek model. Now I'm ready to try the Redeemer model." People came to us because they knew we were thriving in one of the least churched, most secular cities in the U.S. But when visitors first started coming to Redeemer in the early and mid-1990s, they were disappointed because they did not discern a new "model"—at least not in the form of unique, new programs. That's because the real "secret" of Redeemer's fruitfulness does not lie in its ministry programs but in something that functions at a deeper level.

Hardware, Middleware, Software

What was this deeper level, exactly? As time went on, I began to realize it was a middle space between these two more obvious dimensions of ministry. All of us have a *doctrinal foundation*—a set of theological beliefs—and all of us conduct particular *forms of ministry*. But many ministers take up programs and practices of ministry that fit well with neither their doctrinal beliefs nor their cultural context. They adopt popular methods that are essentially "glued on" from the outside—alien to the church's theology or setting (sometimes both!). And when this happens, we find a lack of fruitfulness. These ministers don't change people's lives within the church and don't reach people in their city. Why not? Because the programs do not grow naturally out of reflection on both the gospel and the distinctness of their surrounding culture.

If you think of your doctrinal foundation as "hardware" and of ministry programs as "software," it is important to understand the existence of something called "middleware." I am no computer expert, but my computer-savvy friends tell me that middleware is a software layer that lies between the hardware and the operating system and the various software applications being deployed by the computer's user. In the same way, between one's doctrinal beliefs and ministry practices should be a well-conceived vision for how to bring the gospel to bear on the particular cultural setting and historical moment. This is something more practical than just doctrinal beliefs but much more theological than how-to steps for carrying out a particular ministry. Once this vision is in place, with its emphases and values, it leads church leaders to make good decisions on how to worship, disciple, evangelize, serve, and engage culture in their field of ministry—whether in a city, suburb, or small town.

Theological Vision

This middleware is similar to what Richard Lints, professor of theology at Gordon-Conwell Theological Seminary, calls a "theological vision."[1] According to Lints, our doctrinal foundation, drawn from Scripture, is the starting point for everything:

> Theology must first be about a conversation with God ... God speaks and we listen ... The Christian theological framework is primarily about listening—listening to God. One of the great dangers we face in doing theology is our desire to do all the talking ... We most often capitulate to this temptation by placing alien conceptual boundaries on what God can and has said in the Word ... We force the message of redemption into a cultural package that distorts its actual intentions. Or we attempt to view the gospel solely from the perspective of a tradition that has little living connection to the redemptive work of Christ on the cross. Or we place rational restrictions on the very notion of God instead of allowing God to define the notions of rationality.[2]

However, the doctrinal foundation is not enough. Before you choose specific ministry methods, you must first ask how your doctrinal beliefs "might relate to the modern world." The result of that question "thereby form[s] a theological vision."[3] In other words, a theological vision is a vision for what you are going to *do* with your doctrine in a particular time and place. And what does a theological vision develop from? Lints shows that it comes, of course, from deep reflection on the Bible itself, but it also depends a great deal on what you think of the culture around you. Lints offers this important observation:

> A theological vision allows [people] to see their culture in a way different than they had ever been able to see it before ... Those who are empowered by the theological vision do not simply stand against the mainstream impulses of the culture but take the initiative both to understand and speak to that culture from the framework of the Scriptures ... The modern theological vision must seek to bring the entire counsel of God into the world of its time in order that its time might be transformed.[4]

In light of this, I propose a set of questions that can guide us in the development of a theological vision. As we answer questions like these, a theological vision will emerge:

- What is the gospel, and how do we bring it to bear on the hearts of people today?
- What is this culture like, and how can we both connect to it and challenge it in our communication?
- Where are we located—city, suburb, town, rural area—and how does this affect our ministry?
- To what degree and how should Christians be involved in civic life and cultural production?
- How do the various ministries in a church—word and deed, community and instruction—relate to one another?
- How innovative will our church be and how traditional?
- How will our church relate to other churches in our city and region?

- How will we make our case to the culture about the truth of Christianity?

Our theological vision, growing out of our doctrinal foundation but including implicit or explicit readings of culture, is the most immediate cause of our decisions and choices regarding ministry expression. It is a faithful restatement of the gospel with rich implications for life, ministry, and mission in a type of culture at a moment in history. Perhaps we can diagram it like this (see figure):

Center Church

This book was originally published in 2012 as one of three sections of a longer work called *Center Church*. In that book, I presented the theological vision that has guided our ministry at Redeemer. But what did we mean by the term *center church*? We chose this term for several reasons.

1. The gospel is at its center. It is one thing to have a ministry that is gospel-believing and even gospel-proclaiming but quite another to have one that is gospel-centered.

WHAT TO DO

How the gospel is expressed in a particular church in one community at a point in time

- *Local cultural adaptation*
- *Worship style & programming*
- *Discipleship & outreach processes*
- *Church governance & management*

HOW TO SEE

A faithful restatement of the gospel with rich implications for life, ministry, and mission in a type of culture at a moment in history

- *Vision and values*
- *Ministry "DNA"*
- *Emphases, stances*
- *Philosophy of ministry*

WHAT TO BELIEVE

Timeless truths from the Bible about God, our relationship to him, and his purposes in the world

- *Theological tradition*
- *Denominational affiliation*
- *Systematic & biblical theology*

2. The center is the place of balance. We need to strike balances as Scripture does: of word *and* deed ministries; of challenging *and* affirming human culture; of cultural engagement *and* countercultural distinctiveness; of commitment to truth *and* generosity to others who don't share the same beliefs; of tradition *and* innovation in practice.

3. Our theological vision must be shaped by and for urban and cultural centers. Ministry in the center of global cities is the highest priority for the church in the twenty-first century. While our theological vision is widely applicable, it must be distinctly flavored by the urban experience.

4. The theological vision is at the center of ministry. A theological vision creates a bridge between doctrine and expression. It is central to how all ministry happens. Two churches can have different doctrinal frameworks and ministry expressions but the same theological vision — and they will feel like sister ministries. On the other hand, two churches can have similar doctrinal frameworks and ministry expressions but different theological visions — and they will feel distinct.

The Center Church theological vision can be expressed most simply in three basic commitments: Gospel, City, and Movement.[5] Each book in the Center Church series covers one of these three commitments.

Gospel. Both the Bible and church history show us that it is possible to hold all the correct individual biblical doctrines and yet functionally lose our grasp on the gospel. It is critical, therefore, in every new generation and setting to find ways to *communicate the gospel clearly and strikingly*, distinguishing it from its opposites and counterfeits.

City. All churches must understand, love, and identify with their local community and social setting, and yet at the same time be able and willing to critique and challenge it. Every church, whether located in a city, suburb, or rural area (and there are many permutations and combinations of these settings), must become wise about and conversant with the distinctives of human life in those places. But we must also think about how Christianity and the church engage and interact with culture in general. This has become an acute issue as Western culture has become increasingly post-Christian.

Movement. The last area of theological vision has to do with your church's *relationships* — with its community, with its recent and deeper past, and with other churches and ministries. Some churches are highly institutional, with a strong emphasis on their own past, while others are anti-institutional, fluid, and marked by constant innovation and change. Some churches see themselves as being loyal to a particular ecclesiastical tradition—and so they cherish historical and traditional liturgy and ministry practices. Those that identify very strongly with a particular denomination or newer tradition often resist change. At the other end of the spectrum are churches with little sense of a theological and ecclesiastical past that tend to relate easily to a wide variety of other churches and ministries. All of these different perspectives have an enormous impact on how we actually do ministry.

The Balance of Three Axes

One of the simplest ways to convey the need for wisdom and balance in formulating principles of theological vision is to think of three axes.

1. **The Gospel axis.** At one end of the axis is legalism, the teaching that asserts or the spirit that implies we can save ourselves by how we live. At the other end is antinomianism or, in popular parlance, relativism—the view that it doesn't matter how we live; that God, if he exists, loves everyone the same. But the gospel is neither legalism nor relativism. We are saved by faith and grace alone, but not by a faith that remains alone. True grace always results in changed lives of holiness and justice. It is, of course, possible to lose the gospel because of heterodoxy. That is, if we no longer believe in the deity of Christ or the doctrine of justification, we will necessarily slide toward relativism. But it is also possible to hold sound doctrine and yet be marked by dead orthodoxy (a spirit of self-righteousness), imbalanced orthodoxy (overemphasis on some doctrines that obscure the gospel call), or even

"clueless orthodoxy," which results when doctrines are expounded as in a theology class but aren't brought together to penetrate people's hearts so they experience conviction of sin and the beauty of grace. Our communication and practices must not tend toward either law or license. To the degree that they do, they lose life-changing power.[6]

underadapted
only challenge — CITY — overadapted
only appreciate

2. The City axis (which could also be called a Culture axis). We will show that to reach people we must appreciate and adapt to their culture, but we must also challenge and confront it. This is based on the biblical teaching that all cultures have God's grace and natural revelation in them, yet they are also in rebellious idolatry. If we overadapt to a culture, we have accepted the culture's idols. If, however, we underadapt to a culture, we may have turned our own culture into an idol, an absolute. If we overadapt to a culture, we aren't able to change people because we are not calling them to change. If we underadapt to a culture, no one will be changed because no one will listen to us; we will be confusing, offensive, or simply unpersuasive. To the degree a ministry is overadapted or underadapted to a culture, it loses life-changing power.

structured organization
tradition and authority — MOVEMENT — fluid organism
cooperation and unity

3. The Movement axis. Some churches identify so strongly with their own theological tradition that they cannot make common cause with other evangelical churches or other institutions to reach a city or work for the common good. They also tend to cling strongly to forms of ministry from the past and are highly structured and institutional. Other churches are strongly anti-institutional. They have almost no identification with a particular heritage or denomination, nor do they have much of a relationship to a Christian past. Sometimes they have virtually no institutional character, being completely fluid and informal. A church at either extreme will stifle the development of leadership and strangle the health of the church as a corporate body, as a community. To the degree that it commits either of these errors, it loses its life-giving power.

The more that ministry comes "from the center" of all the axes, the more dynamism and fruitfulness it will have. Ministry that is toward the end of any of the spectrums or axes will drain a ministry of life-changing power with the people in and around it.

As with the original publication of *Center Church*, my hope is that each of these smaller volumes will be useful and provoke discussion. The three volumes of the paperback series each correspond to one of the three axes.

Shaped by the Gospel looks at the need to recover a biblical view of the gospel. Our churches must be characterized by our gospel-theological depth rather than by our doctrinal shallowness, pragmatism, nonreflectiveness, and method-driven philosophy. In addition, we need to experience renewal so that a constant note of grace is applied to everything and our ministry is not marked by legalism or cold intellectualism.

Loving the City highlights the need to be sensitive to culture rather than choosing to ignore our cultural moment or being oblivious to cultural differences among groups. It looks at how we can develop a vision for our city by adopting city-loving ways of ministry rather than approaches that are hostile or indifferent to the city. We also look at how to engage the culture in such a way that we avoid being either too triumphalistic or too withdrawn and subcultural in our attitude.

Serving a Movement shows why every ministry of the church should be outward facing, expecting the presence of nonbelievers and supporting laypeople in their ministry in the world. We also look at the need for integrative ministry where we minister in word *and* deed, helping to meet the spiritual and physical needs of the poor as well as those who live and work in cultural centers. Finally, we look at the need for a mind-set of willing cooperation with other believers, not being turf conscious and suspicious but eagerly promoting a vision for the whole city.

The purpose of these three volumes, then, is not to lay out a "Redeemer model." This is not a "church in a box." Instead, we are laying out a particular theological vision for ministry that we believe will enable many churches to reach people in our day and time, particularly where late-modern Western globalization is influencing the culture. This is especially true in the great cities of the world, but these cultural shifts are being felt everywhere, and so we trust that this book will be found useful to church leaders in a great variety of social settings. We will be recommending a vision for using the gospel in the lives of contemporary people, doing contextualization, understanding cities, doing cultural engagement, discipling for mission, integrating various ministries, and fostering movement dynamics in your congregation and in the world. This set of emphases and values — a Center Church theological vision — can empower all kinds of church models and methods in all kinds of settings. We believe that if you embrace the process of making your theological vision visible, you will make far better choices of model and method.

A NOTE FROM TIMOTHY KELLER

Center Church is a textbook for church leaders working at ministry today, especially for those in urban or urbanized areas. This volume consists of material from the first two parts of *Center Church*, namely, Gospel Theology and Gospel Renewal, together with two essays by other authors giving their reflections on the content, followed by my responses to their reflections. The two authors presenting very fine essays here are Michael Horton, who reflects on Gospel Theology, and Dane Ortlund, who reflects on Gospel Renewal.

The thesis of *Center Church* is that the gospel is not just the minimum set of beliefs required for salvation. All ministry must be resourced, shaped, and directed by the gospel. Therefore the content in Gospel Theology and, to some degree, in Gospel Renewal is foundational to all that comes after. We have to come to grips with what the gospel is before we can apply it to every area of the church's ministry.

As you will see in this volume, I have outlined my response essays using three headings — Grateful, Helpful, and Intriguing. In both essays, there were many places where the author confirmed some of the theses of *Center Church* and often strengthened them with supplemental arguments and examples. For these affirmations I am grateful. There were also places where each author offered critiques or pushbacks. Invariably I found these criticisms very helpful.

Either I agreed and simply said, "You are right." Or I disagreed in part but still learned about things I should do differently—things I share with the reader. Finally, I have a category of "I don't think so, yet your proposals are intriguing." In other words, while I don't agree with their critiques, the issues they raise are very fruitful for further reflection. I take some time to do that reflection and pluck some of the fruit.

I will reserve almost all of what I have to say until later (in my specific responses to the essays). But there are two top-level lessons from these interactions that I can summarize and present here. The first is that *Center Church* is too short. Now that sounds like a ludicrous thing to say about a volume of more than 200,000 words and scores of sidebars and hundreds of tiny-font chapter endnotes. In one sense, it *is* quite long, and this new series that breaks it into multiple volumes is testimony to that. Yet because *Center Church* covers so much territory, I found that many of the critiques called for content to be included that actually exists elsewhere. Much of what Dane Ortlund misses in the Gospel Renewal chapters can be found in the book *Preaching: Communicating Faith in an Age of Skepticism*. Other essayists will complain that certain theses and arguments need to be made, which exist in books like *Generous Justice: How God's Grace Makes Us Just* and *Every Good Endeavor: Connecting Your Work to God's Work*. These essays help me see that these supplementary texts are more important than I thought for equipping people to do ministry today and must not be overlooked.

The second lesson I am learning is that I am a practitioner first—a working preacher and pastor—not a theologian. That means my actual practice of ministry is more complete than my theoretical description of it. A number of times an essayist writes something like this: "Keller says *this*, but he never brings in and connects it to *that*." Often they add, kindly, "I know he does this in his preaching, but I don't see it here." Like many practitioners, I can do something with a fair amount of skillfulness but then have trouble explaining what I did or how someone else can do it. Some of the essays have shown me specific places where I have fallen short in this regard.

All this is to say that the essays greatly enhance the value of the material now in your hands. I hope the give-and-take of the dialogue and the additional insights, as well as the original material, will make this a valuable training tool for equipping Christians for ministry in an increasingly complex world.

Part 1

GOSPEL
THEOLOGY

Chapter 1

THE GOSPEL
IS NOT
EVERYTHING

What do we mean by "the gospel"? Answering this question is a bit more complex than we often assume. Not everything the Bible teaches can be considered "the gospel" (although it can be argued that all biblical doctrine is necessary background for understanding the gospel). The gospel is a *message* about how we have been rescued from peril. The very word *gospel* has as its background a news report about some life-altering event that has already happened.[1]

1. The gospel is good news, not good advice. The gospel is not primarily a way of life. It is not something we do, but something that has been done for us and something that we must respond to. In the Greek translation of the Old Testament—the Septuagint—the word *euangelizō* (proclaim good news) occurs twenty-three times. As we see in Psalm 40:9 (ESV)—"I have told the glad news of [your] deliverance in the great congregation"—the term is generally used to declare the news of something that has happened to rescue and deliver people from peril. In the New Testament, the word group *euangelion (*good news), *euangelizō* (proclaim good news), and *euangelistēs* (one who proclaims good news) occurs at least 133 times. D. A. Carson draws this conclusion from a thorough study of gospel words:

> Because the gospel is news, good news . . . it is to be announced; that is what one does with news. The essential heraldic element

in preaching is bound up with the fact that the core message is not a code of ethics to be debated, still less a list of aphorisms to be admired and pondered, and certainly not a systematic theology to be outlined and schematized. Though it properly grounds ethics, aphorisms, and systematics, it is none of these three: it is news, good news, and therefore must be publicly announced.[2]

2. The gospel is good news announcing that we have been rescued or saved. And what are we rescued *from*? What peril are we saved from? A look at the gospel words in the New Testament shows that we are rescued from "the coming wrath" at the end of history (1 Thess 1:10). But this wrath is not an impersonal force—it is God's wrath. We are out of fellowship with God; our relationship with him is broken.

In perhaps the most thoroughgoing exposition of the gospel in the Bible, Paul identifies God's wrath as the great problem of the human condition (Rom 1:18–32). Here we see that the wrath of God has many ramifications. The background text is Genesis 3:17–19, in which God's curse lies on the entire created order because of human sin. Because we are alienated from God, we are *psychologically* alienated within ourselves—we experience shame and fear (Gen 3:10). Because we are alienated from God, we are also *socially* alienated from one another (v. 7 describes how Adam and Eve must put on clothing, and v. 16 speaks of alienation between the genders; also notice the blame shifting in their dialogue with God in vv. 11–13). Because we are alienated from God, we are also *physically* alienated from nature itself. We now experience sorrow, painful toil, physical degeneration, and death (vv. 16–19). In fact, the ground itself is "cursed" (v. 17; see Rom 8:18–25).

Since the garden, we live in a world filled with suffering, disease, poverty, racism, natural disasters, war, aging, and death—and it all stems from the wrath and curse of God on the world. The world is out of joint, and we need to be rescued. But the root of our problem is not these "horizontal" relationships, though they are often the most obvious; it is our "vertical" relationship with God. All human problems are ultimately symptoms, and our separation from God is the cause. The reason for all the misery—all the effects of the curse—is that we are not reconciled to God. We see this in such texts as Romans 5:8 and 2 Corinthians 5:20. Therefore, the first and primary focus of any real rescue of the human race—the main thing that will save us—is to have our relationship with God put right again.

3. The gospel is news about what has been done by Jesus Christ to put right our relationship with God. Becoming a Christian is about a change of status. First John 3:14 (emphasis added) states that "we *have passed* from death to life," not we *are passing* from death to life.[3] You are either in Christ or you are not; you are either pardoned and accepted or you are not; you either have eternal life or you don't. This is why Dr. Martyn Lloyd-Jones often used a diagnostic question to determine a person's spiritual understanding and condition. He would ask, "Are you now ready to say that you are a Christian?" He recounts that over the years, whenever he would ask the question, people would often hesitate and then say, "I do not feel that I am good enough." To that, he gives this response: "At once I know that ... they are still thinking in terms of themselves; their idea still is that they have to make themselves good enough to be a Christian ... It sounds very modest but it is the lie of the devil, it is a denial of the faith ... you will never be good enough; nobody has ever been good enough. The essence of the Christian salvation is to say that He is good enough and that I am in Him!"[4]

Lloyd-Jones's point is that becoming a Christian is a change in our relationship with God. Jesus' work, when it is believed and rested in, instantly changes our standing before God. We are "in him."

Ever since reading J. I. Packer's famous essay introducing John Owen's *The Death of Death in the Death of Christ*, I have liked "God saves sinners" as a good summary of gospel:

> God saves sinners. God—the Triune Jehovah, Father, Son and Spirit; three Persons working together in sovereign wisdom, power and love to achieve the salvation of a chosen people, the Father electing, the Son fulfilling the Father's will by redeeming, the Spirit executing the purpose of Father and Son by renewing. Saves—does everything, first to last, that is involved in bringing man from death in sin to life in glory: plans, achieves and communicates redemption, calls and keeps, justifies, sanctifies, glorifies. Sinners—men as God finds them, guilty, vile, helpless, powerless, unable to lift a finger to do God's will or better their spiritual lot.[5]

The Gospel Is Not the Results of the Gospel

The gospel is not about something we do but about what has been done for us, and yet the gospel results in a whole new way of life. This grace and the good deeds that result must be both distinguished and connected. The gospel, its results, and its implications must be carefully related to each other—neither confused nor separated. One of Martin Luther's dicta was that we are saved by faith alone but not by a faith that remains alone. His point is that true gospel belief will always and necessarily lead to good works, but salvation in no way comes through or because of good works. Faith and works must never be confused for one another, nor may they be separated (Eph 2:8–10; Jas 2:14, 17–18, 20, 22, 24, 26).

I am convinced that belief in the gospel leads us to care for the poor and participate actively in our culture, as surely as Luther said true faith leads to good works. But just as faith and works must not be separated or confused, so the results of the gospel must never be separated from or confused with the gospel itself. I have often heard people preach this way: "The good news is that God *is* healing and *will* heal the world of all its hurts; therefore, the work of the gospel is to work for justice and peace in the world." The danger in this line of thought is not that the particulars are untrue (they are not) but that it mistakes effects for causes. It confuses what the gospel *is* with what the gospel *does*. When Paul speaks of the renewed material creation, he states that the new heavens and new earth are guaranteed to us because on the cross Jesus restored our relationship with God as his true sons and daughters. Romans 8:1–25 teaches, remarkably, that the redemption of our bodies and of the entire physical world occurs when we receive "our adoption." As his children, we are guaranteed our future inheritance (Eph 1:13–14, 18; Col 1:12; 3:24; Heb 9:15; 1 Pet 1:4), and *because* of that inheritance, the world is renewed. The *future* is ours because of Christ's work finished in the *past*.

We must not, then, give the impression that the gospel is simply a divine rehabilitation program for the world, but rather that it is an accomplished substitutionary work. We must not depict the gospel as primarily *joining* something (Christ's kingdom program) but rather as *receiving* something (Christ's finished work). If we make this error, the gospel becomes another kind of a salvation by works instead of a salvation by faith. As J. I. Packer writes, "The gospel does bring us solutions to these problems [of suffering and injustice], but it does so by first solving ... the deepest of all human problems, the problem of man's relation with his Maker; and unless we make it plain that the solution of these former problems depends on the settling of this latter one, we are misrepresenting the message and becoming false witnesses of God."[6]

A related question has to do with whether the gospel is spread by the doing of justice. Not only does the Bible say over and over that the gospel is spread by preaching, but common sense tells us that loving deeds, as important as they are as an accompaniment of preaching, cannot by themselves bring people to a saving knowledge of Jesus Christ. Francis Schaeffer argued rightly that Christians' relationships with each other constitute the criterion the world uses to judge whether their message is truthful — so Christian community is the "final apologetic."[7] Notice again, however, the relationship between faith and works. Jesus said that a loving community is necessary for the world to know that God sent him (John 17:23; cf. 13:35). Sharing our goods with each other and with the needy is a powerful sign to nonbelievers (see the relationship between witness and sharing in Acts 4:31–37 and Acts 6). But loving deeds — even though they embody the truths of the gospel and cannot be separated from preaching the gospel — should not be conflated with it.

The gospel, then, is preeminently a report about the work of Christ on our behalf — that is why and how the gospel is salvation by grace. The gospel is news because it is about a salvation accomplished for us. It is news that creates a life of love, but the life of love is not itself the gospel.[8]

The Gospel Has Two Equal and Opposite Enemies

The ancient church father Tertullian is reputed to have said, "Just as Jesus was crucified between two thieves, so the gospel is ever crucified between these two errors."[9] What are these errors to which Tertullian was referring? I often call them *religion* and *irreligion*; the theological terms are *legalism* and *antinomianism*. Another way to describe them could be *moralism* and *relativism* (or *pragmatism*).

These two errors constantly seek to corrupt the message and steal away from us the power of the gospel. Legalism says that we have to live a holy, good life in order to be saved. Antinomianism says that because we are saved, we don't have to live a holy, good life.

This is the location of the "tip of the spear" of the gospel. A very clear and sharp distinction between legalism, antinomianism, and the gospel is often crucial for the life-changing power of the Holy Spirit to work. If our gospel message even slightly resembles "you must believe and live right to be saved" *or* "God loves and accepts everyone just as they are," we will find our communication is not doing the identity-changing, heart-shaping transformative work described in the next part of this book. If we just preach general doctrine and ethics from Scripture, we are not preaching the gospel. The gospel is the good news that God has accomplished our salvation for us through Christ in order to bring us into a right relationship with him and eventually to destroy all the results of sin in the world.

Still, it can be rightly argued that in order to understand all this—who God is, why we need salvation, what he has done to save us—we must have knowledge of the basic teachings of the entire Bible. J. Gresham Machen, for example, speaks of the biblical doctrines of God and of man to be the "presuppositions of the gospel."[10] This means that an understanding of the Trinity, of Christ's incarnation, of original sin and sin in general—are all necessary. If we don't understand, for example, that Jesus was not just a good man but the second person of the Trinity, or if we don't understand what the "wrath of God" means, it is impossible to understand what Jesus accomplished on the cross. Not only that, but the New Testament constantly explains the work of Christ in Old Testament terms—in the language of priesthood, sacrifice, and covenant.

In other words, we must *not* just preach the Bible in general; we must preach the gospel. Yet unless those listening to the message understand the Bible in general, they won't grasp the gospel. The more we understand the whole corpus of biblical doctrine, the more we will understand the gospel itself—and the more we understand the gospel, the more we will come to see that this is, in the end, what the Bible is really about. Biblical knowledge is necessary for the gospel *and* distinct from the gospel, yet it so often stands in when the gospel is not actually present that people have come to mistake its identity.

The Gospel Has Chapters

So, the gospel is good news—it is not something we do but something that has been done for us. Simple enough. But when we ask questions like "Good news about what?" or "Why is it good news?" the richness and complexity of the gospel begin to emerge.

There are two basic ways to answer the question "What is the gospel?" One is to offer the biblical good news of how you can get right with God. This is to understand the question to mean, "What must *I* do to be saved?" The second is to offer the biblical good news of what God will fully accomplish in history through the salvation of Jesus. This is to understand the question as "What hope is there for the world?"

If we conceive the question in the first, more individualistic way, we explain how a sinful human being can be reconciled to a holy God and how his or her life can be changed as a result. It is a message about *individuals*. The answer can be outlined: Who God is, what sin is, who Christ is and what he did, and what faith is. These are basically propositions. If we conceive of the question in the second way, to ask all that God is going to accomplish in history, we explain where the world came from, what went wrong with it, and what must happen for it to be mended. This is a message about the *world*. The answer can be outlined: creation, fall, redemption, and restoration. These are chapters in a plotline, a story.

As we will see in the next chapter, there is no single way to present the biblical gospel. Yet I urge you to try to be as thoughtful as possible in your gospel presentations. The danger in answering only the first question ("What must I do to be saved?") without the second ("What hope is there for the world?") is that, standing alone, the first can play into the Western idea that religion exists to provide spiritual goods that meet individual spiritual needs for freedom from guilt and bondage. It does not speak much about the goodness of the original creation or of God's concern for the material world, and so this conception may set up the listener to see Christianity as sheer escape from the world. But the danger in conceiving the gospel too strictly as a story line of the renewal of the world is even greater. It tells listeners about God's program to save the world, but it does not tell them how to actually get right with God and become part of that program. In fact, I'll say that without the first message, the second message is not the gospel. J. I. Packer writes these words:

> In recent years, great strides in biblical theology and contemporary canonical exegesis have brought new precision to our grasp of the Bible's overall story of how God's plan to bless Israel, and through Israel the world, came to its climax in and through Christ. But I do not see how it can be denied that each New Testament book, whatever other job it may be doing, has in view, one way or another, Luther's primary question: how may a weak, perverse, and guilty sinner find a gracious God? Nor can it be denied that real Christianity only really starts when that discovery is made. And to the extent that modern developments, by filling our horizon with the great metanarrative, distract us from pursuing Luther's question in personal terms, they hinder as well as help in our appreciation of the gospel.[11]

Still, the Bible's grand narrative of cosmic redemption is critical background to help an individual get right with God. One way to proceed is to interleave the two answers to the "What is the gospel?" question so that gospel truths are laid into a story with chapters rather than just presented as a set of propositions. The narrative approach poses the questions, and the propositional approach supplies the answers.

How would we relate the gospel to someone in this way? What follows is a "conversational pathway" for presenting the gospel to someone as the chapters in a story. In the Bible, the term *gospel* is the declaration of what Jesus Christ has done to save us. In light of the biblical usage, then, we should observe that chapters 1 (God and Creation), 2 (Fall and Sin), and 4 (Faith) are not, strictly speaking, "the gospel." They are prologue and epilogue. Simon Gathercole argues that both Paul and the Gospel writers considered the good news to have three basic elements: the identity of Jesus as Son of God and Messiah, the death of Jesus for sin and justification, and the establishment of the reign of God and the new creation.[12] The gospel, then, is packed into chapter 3, with its three headings — incarnation, substitution, and restoration. Chapter 1 on God and chapter 2 on sin constitute absolutely critical background information for understanding the meaning of the person and work of Jesus, and chapter 4 helps us understand how we must respond to Jesus' salvation. Nevertheless, it is reasonable and natural to refer to the entire set of four chapters as "the gospel."

CHAPTERS	GOSPEL NARRATIVE	GOSPEL TRUTHS
Chapter 1	Where did we come from?	God: the One and the relational
Chapter 2	Why did things go so wrong?	Sin: bondage and condemnation
Chapter 3	What will put things right?	Christ: incarnation, substitution, restoration
Chapter 4	How can I be put right?	Faith: grace and trust

Where Did We Come From?

Answer: God. There is one God. He is infinite in power, goodness, and holiness and yet also personal and loving, a God who speaks to us in the Bible. The world is not an accident, but the creation of the one God (Genesis 1). God created all things, but *why* did he do that? Why did he create the world and us? The answer is what makes the Christian understanding of God profound and unique. While there is only one God, within God's being there are three persons—Father, Son, and Holy Spirit—who are all equally God and who have loved, adored, served, and enjoyed one another from all eternity. If God were uni-personal, then he would have not known love until he created other beings. In that case, love and community would not have been essential to his character; it would have emerged later. But God is triune, and therefore love, friendship, and community are intrinsic to him and at the heart of all reality. So a triune God created us (John 1:1–4), but he would not have created us to get the joy of mutual love and service, because he already had that. Rather, he created us to share in his love and service. As we know from John 17:20–24, the persons of the Trinity love and serve one another—they are "other-oriented."[13] And thus God created us to live in the same way. In order to share the joy and love that God knew within himself, he created a good world that he cares for, a world full of human beings who were called to worship, know, and serve him, not themselves.[14]

Why Did Things Go So Wrong?

Answer: Sin. God created us to adore and serve him and to love others. By living this way, we would have been completely happy and enjoyed a perfect world. But instead, the whole human race turned away from God, rebelling against his authority. Instead of living for God and our neighbors, we live lives of self-centeredness. Because our relationship with God has been broken, all other relationships—with other human beings, with our very selves, and with the created world—are also ruptured. The result is spiritual, psychological, social, and physical decay and breakdown. "Things fall apart; the center cannot hold. Mere anarchy is loosed upon the world"[15]—the world now lies under the power of sin.

Sin reaps two terrible consequences. One consequence is spiritual bondage (Rom 6:15–18). We may believe in God or we may not believe, but either way, we never make him our greatest hope, good, or love. We try to maintain control of our lives by living for other things—for money, career, family, fame, romance, sex, power, comfort, social and political causes, or something else. But the result is always a loss of control, a form of slavery. Everyone has to live for something, and if that something is not God, then we are driven by that thing we live for—by overwork to achieve it, by inordinate fear if it is threatened, deep anger if it is being blocked, and inconsolable despair if it is lost. So the novelist David Foster Wallace, not long before his suicide, spoke these words to the 2005 graduating class at Kenyon College:

> Everybody worships. The only choice we get is what to worship. And the compelling reason for maybe choosing some sort of god or spiritual-type thing to worship ... is that pretty much anything else you worship will eat you alive. If you worship money and things, if they are where you tap real meaning in life, then you will never have enough, never feel you have enough ... Worship your body and beauty and sexual allure and you will always feel ugly. And when time and age start showing, you will die a million deaths before they finally grieve you ... Worship power, you will end up feeling weak and afraid, and you will need ever more power over others to numb you to your own fear. Worship your intellect, being seen as smart,

you will end up feeling stupid, a fraud, always on the verge of being found out. But the insidious thing about these forms of worship is ... they're unconscious. They are default settings.[16]

The second basic consequence of sin is condemnation (Rom 6:23). We are not just suffering because of sin; we are *guilty* because of sin. Often we say, "Well, I'm not very religious, but I'm a good person—and that is what is most important." But is it? Imagine a woman—a poor widow—with an only son. She teaches him how she wants him to live—to always tell the truth, to work hard, and to help the poor. She makes very little money, but with her meager savings she is able to put him through college. Imagine that when he graduates, he hardly ever speaks to her again. He occasionally sends a Christmas card, but he doesn't visit her; he won't answer her phone calls or letters; he doesn't speak to her. But he lives just like she taught him—honestly, industriously, and charitably. Would we say this was acceptable? Of course not! Wouldn't we say that by living a "good life" but neglecting a relationship with the one to whom he owed everything he was doing something condemnable? In the same way, if God created us and we owe him everything and we do not live for him but we "live a good life," it is not enough. We all owe a debt that must be paid.

What Will Put Things Right?

Answer: Christ. First, Jesus Christ puts things right through his *incarnation*. C. S. Lewis wrote that if there is a God, we certainly don't relate to him as people on the first floor of a building relate to people on the second floor. We relate to him the way Hamlet relates to Shakespeare. We (characters) might be able to know quite a lot about the playwright, but only to the degree that the author chooses to put information about himself in the play.[17]

In the Christian view, however, we believe that God did even more than simply give us information. Many fans of Dorothy Sayers's detective stories and mystery novels point out that Sayers was one of the first women to attend Oxford University. The main character in her stories—Lord Peter Wimsey—is an aristocratic sleuth and a single man. At one point in the novels, though, a new character appears, Harriet Vane. She is described as one of the first women who graduated from Oxford—and as a writer of mystery novels. Eventually she and Peter fall in love and marry. Who was she? Many believe Sayers looked into the world she had created, fell in love with her lonely hero, and wrote herself into the story to save him. Very touching! But that is not nearly as moving or amazing as the reality of the incarnation (John 1:14). God, as it were, looked into the world he had made and saw our lostness and had pity on his people. And so he wrote *himself* into human history as its main character (John 3:16). The second person in the Trinity, the Son of God, came into the world as a man, Jesus Christ.

The second way Jesus puts things right is through *substitution*. Because of the guilt and condemnation on us, a just God can't simply shrug off our sins. Being sorry is not enough. We would never allow an earthly judge to let a wrongdoer off, just because he was contrite—how much less should we expect a perfect heavenly Judge to do so? And even when we forgive personal wrongs against us, we cannot simply forgive without cost. If someone harms us and takes money or happiness or reputation from us, we can either make them pay us back or forgive them—which means *we* absorb the cost ourselves without remuneration. Jesus Christ lived a perfect life—the only human being to ever do so (Heb 4:15). At the end of his life, he deserved blessing and acceptance; at the end of our lives, because every one of us lives in sin, we deserve rejection and condemnation (Rom 3:9–10). Yet when the time had fully come, Jesus received in our place, on the cross, the rejection and condemnation we deserve (1 Pet 3:18), so that, when we believe in him, we can receive the blessing and acceptance he deserves (2 Cor 5:21).

There is no more moving thought than that of someone giving his life to save another. In Charles Dickens's *A Tale of Two Cities*, two men—Charles Darnay and Sydney Carton—both love the same woman, Lucie Manette, but Lucie chooses to marry Charles. Later, during the French Revolution, Charles is thrown in prison and awaits execution on the guillotine. Sydney visits Charles in prison, drugs him, and has him carried out. When a young seamstress (also on death row) realizes that Sydney is taking Charles's place, she is amazed and asks him to hold her hand for strength. She is deeply moved by his substitutionary sacrifice—and it wasn't even for her! When we realize that Jesus did the very same thing for us, it changes everything—the way we regard God, ourselves, and the world.

The third way Jesus will put things right is through the eventual *restoration* of all that has gone wrong with the world. The first time Jesus came from heaven to earth, he came in weakness to suffer for our sins. But the second time he comes, he will judge the world, putting a final end to all evil, suffering, decay, and death (Rom 8:19–21; 2 Pet 3:13). This means that Christ's salvation does not merely save our souls so we can escape the pain of the curse on the physical world. Rather, the final goal is the renewal and restoration of the material world, and the redemption of both our souls *and* our bodies. Vinoth Ramachandra notes how unique this view is among the religions of the world:

> So our salvation lies not in an escape from this world but in the transformation of this world ... You will not find hope for the world in any religious systems or philosophies of humankind. The biblical vision is unique. That is why when some say that there is salvation in other faiths I ask them, "What salvation are you talking about?" No faith holds out a promise of eternal salvation for the world the way the cross and resurrection of Jesus do.[18]

How Can I Be Put Right?

Answer: Faith. Jesus died for our sins and rose again from the grave. By faith in him, our sins can be forgiven and we can be assured of living forever with God and one day being raised from the dead like Christ. So what does it mean to believe, to have faith? First, it means to grasp what salvation "by faith" means. Believing in Christ does not mean that we are forgiven for our past, get a new start on life, and must simply try harder to live better than we did in the past. If this is your mind-set, you are still putting your faith in yourself. You are your own Savior. You are looking to your moral efforts and abilities to make yourself right with God. But this will never work. No one lives a perfect life. Even your best deeds are tainted by selfish and impure motives.

The gospel is that when we believe in Christ, there is now "no condemnation for those who are in Christ Jesus" (Rom 8:1). Putting our faith in Christ is not about trying harder; it means *transferring our trust* away from ourselves and resting in him. It means saying, "Father, accept me not because of what I have done or ever will do but because of what Jesus has done in my place." When we do that, we are adopted into God's family and given the right to his eternal, fatherly love (John 1:12–13).

The second thing to keep in mind is that it is not the quality of the faith itself that saves us; it is what Jesus has done for us. It is easy to assume that being "saved by faith" means that God will now love us *because* of the depth of our repentance and faith. But that is to once again subtly make ourselves our own Savior rather than Jesus. It is not the amount of our faith but the object of our faith that saves us. Imagine two people boarding an airplane. One person has almost no faith in the plane or the crew and is filled with fears and doubts. The other has great confidence in the plane and the crew. They both enter the plane, fly to a destination, and get off the plane safely. One person had a hundred times more faith in the plane than the other did, but they were equally safe. It wasn't the amount of their faith but the object of their faith (the plane and crew) that kept them from suffering harm and arriving safely at their destination. Saving faith isn't a level of psychological certainty; it is an act of the will in which we rest in Jesus. We give ourselves wholly to him because he gave himself wholly for us (Mark 8:34; Rev 3:20).

The Right Relationship of the Gospel to All of Ministry

There is always a danger that church leaders and ministers will conceive of the gospel as merely the minimum standard of doctrinal content for being a Christian believer. As a result, many preachers and leaders are energized by thoughts of teaching more advanced doctrine, or of deeper forms of spirituality, or of intentional community and the sacraments, or of "deeper discipleship," or of psychological healing, or of social justice and cultural engagement. One of the reasons is the natural emergence of specialization as a church grows and ages. People naturally want to go deeper into various topics and ministry disciplines. But this tendency can cause us to lose sight of the whole. Though we may have an area or a ministry that we tend to focus on, the gospel is what brings unity to all that we do. Every form of ministry is empowered by the gospel, based on the gospel, and is a result of the gospel.

Perhaps an illustration here will help. Imagine you're in an orchestra and you begin to play, but the sound is horrific because the instruments are out of tune. The problem can't be fixed by simply tuning them to each other. It won't help for each person to get in tune to the person next to her because each person will be tuning to something different. No, they will all need to be tuned properly to one source of pitch. Often we go about trying to tune ourselves to the sound of everything else in our lives. We often hear this described as "getting balance." But the questions that need to be asked are these: "Balanced to what?" "Tuned to what?" The gospel does not begin by tuning us in relation to our particular problems and surroundings; it first re-tunes us to God.[19]

If an element of ministry is not recognized as a *result* of the gospel, it may sometimes be mistaken *for* the gospel and eventually supplant the gospel in the church's preaching and teaching. Counseling, spiritual direction, doing justice, engaging culture, doctrinal instruction, and even evangelism itself may become the main thing instead of the gospel. In such cases, the gospel as outlined above is no longer understood as the fountainhead, the central dynamic, from which all other things proceed. It is no longer the center of the preaching, the thinking, or the life of the church; some other good thing has replaced it. As a consequence, conversions will begin to dwindle in number because the gospel is not preached with a kind of convicting sharpness that lays bare the secrets of the heart (1 Cor 14:24–25) and gives believers *and* nonbelievers a sense of God's reality, even against their wills.

Because the gospel is endlessly rich, it can handle the burden of being the one "main thing" of a church. First Peter 1:12 and its context indicate that the angels never tire of looking into and exploring the wonders of the gospel. It can be preached from innumerable stories, themes, and principles from all over the Bible. But when the preaching of the gospel is either confused with or separated from the other endeavors of the church, preaching becomes mere exhortation (to get with the church's program or a biblical standard of ethics) or informational instruction (to inculcate the church's values and beliefs). When the proper connection between the gospel and any aspect of ministry is severed, *both* are shortchanged.

● ● ●

The gospel is "heraldic proclamation" before it is anything else.[20] It is news that creates a life of love, but the life of love is not itself the gospel. The gospel is *not* everything that we believe, do, or say. The gospel must primarily be understood as good news, and the news is not as much about what we must do as about what has been done. The gospel is preeminently a report about the work of Christ on our behalf—salvation accomplished for us. That's how it is a gospel of grace. Yet, as we will see in the next chapter, the fact that the gospel is news does not mean it is a *simple* message. There is no such thing as a "one size fits all" understanding of the gospel.

DISCUSSION QUESTIONS

1. This chapter looks at several truths that are not the gospel. In what sense are each of these not the gospel?

   - everything the Bible teaches
   - a way of life; something we do
   - joining Christ's kingdom program; a divine rehabilitation plan for the world

   If the gospel is not everything, what is the gospel?

2. Keller writes, "The gospel is not about something we do but about what has been done for us, and yet the gospel results in a whole new way of life. This grace and the good deeds that result must be both distinguished and connected." How can an individual or ministry go about distinguishing between "the gospel" and "the results of the gospel"?

3. The section titled "The Gospel Has Chapters" shows how to present the gospel to someone as chapters in a larger story. What other conversational pathways have you found to be fruitful in relating the gospel to non-Christians? To Christians?

4. What happens when the gospel is proclaimed without its results, or when its results are pursued without proclamation?

Chapter 2

THE GOSPEL IS NOT A SIMPLE THING

The gospel is not everything, yet in the final analysis it cannot be tamed into a single simple formula with a number of points that must be recited to everyone, in every time and place. There is an irreducible complexity to the gospel. I do not mean that the gospel can't be *presented* simply and even very briefly. Paul himself does so on numerous occasions (e.g., Rom 10:9). The gospel is a clear and present word, but it is not a simplistic word.[1] Though in the previous chapter I gave an example of a gospel outline that I believe is broadly useful today, I want to resist the impulse, mainly among conservative evangelicals, toward creating a single, one-size-fits-all gospel presentation that should be used everywhere, that serves as a test of orthodoxy.

The Bible Doesn't Give One Standard Gospel Outline

In Galatians 1:8, Paul condemns anyone who preaches "a gospel other than the one we preached to you." In 1 Corinthians 15:11, he takes pains to show that the gospel he declares is the same as that preached by Peter, John, and the others: "Whether, then, it is I or they, this is what we preach, and this is what you believed." It would be impossible for Paul to condemn a "false gospel" and affirm the preaching of Peter as "the gospel" without assuming a consensus body of gospel content. And yet it is obvious that the various biblical writers express the gospel in significantly different ways.

For example, when the Synoptic writers speak about the gospel, they constantly use the concept of "the kingdom," but this phrase is virtually missing in John's gospel, which emphasizes, rather, receiving "eternal life." On the one hand, we can say that this difference does not at all constitute a contradiction, because when we compare Matthew 25:31–46 and Mark 10:17–31 with John 3:3–6, 17, we see that entering God's kingdom and receiving eternal life are virtually the same thing. Reading Matthew 18:3; Mark 10:15; and John 3:3–6 together reveals that conversion, the new birth, and receiving the kingdom of God like children are basically the same move.[2]

Nonetheless, the terms *eternal life* and *the kingdom* are not mere synonyms. The Synoptics use *kingdom* so often because their orientation is more toward the future.[3] The terms convey somewhat different aspects of God's salvation. As many have pointed out, John seems to emphasize the individual and the inward aspects of being in the kingdom of God. He takes pains to show that the kingdom is *not* an earthly, sociopolitical order (John 18:36). On the other hand, when the Synoptic writers speak of the kingdom, there is a somewhat more external and corporate emphasis. They lay out the social and behavioral changes that the gospel brings.[4] The kingdom of God *does* take corporate shape, and it *does* have major implications for how we live. It is a new order of things in which money is not made an idol (Mark 10:17–31) and the hungry, naked, and homeless are cared for (Matt 25:31–46). John and the Synoptic writers reveal complementary aspects of the gospel, stressing both the individual and corporate dimensions of our salvation.

So John and the Synoptic writers present the gospel in somewhat different ways. And when we look at the apostle Paul, we find yet another, different set of emphases. While Paul uses both "kingdom" and "life," he more centrally focuses on the concept of justification.

So is this a different gospel? No. Paul stresses the intercanonical theme of the law court. Jesus takes the curse of the law, the legal penalty for sin, so we can receive the blessing of Christ's obedience (Gal 3:13–14). Simon Gathercole has shown that there is no real contradiction between the Synoptic writers, John, and Paul.[5] In Jesus, God substitutes himself for us and, on our behalf, pays the debt (Mark 10:45; John 12:20–36; 1 Tim 2:6); defeats the evil powers (Col 2:15; 1 John 3:8); bears the curse and divine wrath (Matt 27:45; Gal 3:13; 1 John 2:2; 4:10), secures for us salvation by grace, not by our works (Eph 2:8–9; 2 Tim 1:9), and even becomes for us an exemplar (1 Tim 1:16; Heb 12:2; 1 Pet 2:21). At the heart of all of the biblical writers' theology is redemption through substitution.

The Gospel Must Be Tied to the Bible's Story Line and Themes

Over the last several decades, as anthropologists and linguists studied "meaning making" through language in a given society, they began to divide their study into two approaches: a *synchronic* approach, which is concerned with the whole structure of a language at a given time, and a *diachronic* approach, which looks at how language and meaning change as a result of life experience.

Theologians also stress reading the Bible both synchronically and diachronically. The synchronic approach is sometimes called the systematic-theological method (STM), which tends to deal with Scripture topically. It organizes what the Bible says by categories of thought: *The Bible is about God, sin, the Holy Spirit, the church, marriage and family, prayer, and so on.* It looks at every text on a particular topic and synthesizes them into a coherent set of statements or principles. This method is especially sensitive to the Bible's unity in expressing a view of God, humanity, sin, grace, the world, and so on. As I pointed out in the previous chapter, it tends to be particularly useful in answering the gospel question "What must I do to be saved?" We believe we can read the Bible this way because it has a single author—God—and because as rational creatures we respond to the beauty of truth. In this perspective, the gospel appears as *God, sin, Christ,* and *faith.* It brings out the *means* of salvation, namely, the substitutionary work of Christ and our responsibility to embrace it by faith.[6]

To read the Bible diachronically is to read along its narrative arc, and this is often called the redemptive-historical method (RHM), which tends to deal with Scripture historically. It organizes what the Bible says by stages in history or by the plotline of a story: *The Bible is about God's creating the world, the fall of man, God's reentry into history to create a new people for himself, and eventually about a new creation that emerges out of a marred and broken world through Christ.* The method discerns the basic plotline of the Bible as God's story of redemption, as well as the biblical themes (e.g., covenant, kingship, sanctuary) that run through every stage of history and each part of the canon, climaxing in Jesus Christ. This approach is especially sensitive to the differences in historical eras and among biblical authors. It is particularly helpful in answering the gospel question "What hope is there for the world?" We believe we can read the Bible this way because God used human beings to write his revelation—and because as hope-based creatures we respond to the beauty of narrative. In this perspective, the gospel appears as *creation, fall, promise and prefiguration, Israel, Christ's redemption,* and *restoration.* It brings out the *purpose* of salvation, namely, a renewed creation.

There is no ultimate reason these two approaches should contradict one another.[7] In fact, using both approaches does justice to the miraculous fact that the Bible is both unmistakably divine and providentially human. I would go even further and warn that failing to use both approaches invites danger. The STM, carried out in isolation from the RHM, can produce a Christianity that is rationalistic, legalistic, and individualistic. Similarly, the RHM, carried out in isolation from the STM, tends to produce a Christianity that loves narrative and community but shies away from sharp distinctions between grace and law and between truth and heresy.

One approach that draws from both the story line and the themes of Scripture is to read the Bible through *intercanonical themes*. In his essay "The Biblical Gospel," D. A. Carson warns against reductionistic versions of the gospel that do not tie into the Bible's story line.[8] Carson has posited that there may be twenty or so intercanonical themes that hold the Bible together.[9] The gospel unifies and gives meaning to these many threads that run through the Old and New Testaments. A person can explain the gospel from beginning to end through any of these themes, but no single theme gives the full picture.

The table below highlights a few of these. In the next three sections, we will highlight how the gospel can be expressed through each theme.

HOME/EXILE	YAHWEH/ COVENANT	KINGDOM
AT CREATION MADE FOR:		
a place of rest and shalom	a faithful covenant love relationship with God	God's kingdom and kingliness
SIN IS/RESULTS IN:		
self-centeredness, destroying shalom	unfaithfulness, causing God's curse and wrath	idolatry, causing enslavement
ISRAEL IS:		
exiled in Egypt, then Babylon	called to faithfulness but is unfaithful	looking for a true judge/king

JESUS IS:		
the rejected but resurrected Lord, who breaks the power of death	the suffering servant but new covenant Lord, who takes the curse of sin	the returning true king, who frees us from the world, flesh, Devil
RESTORATION:		
the garden-city of God	the marriage supper of the Lamb	true freedom under the reign of God

The Exile and Our Homecoming

Home, according to Scripture, is a place where life flourishes fully—spiritually, physically, and socially. It is a place where physical life and health are sustained and where our most intimate love *relationships* are nurtured. It is place of rest, of shalom.

The story of the human race, however, is one of exile and longing for homecoming. Death and disease have distorted and defaced God's good physical creation. Society is a Babel filled with selfishness, self-exaltation, and pride. Exploitation and violence mar and ruin human community. The world as it now exists is not our true home. We were made for a place without death or parting from love, without decay, and without disease and aging. We are, therefore, exiles and aliens here. Why? Because the human race turned from God to live for itself; our first parents were turned out of the garden of God and banished from the face of God, in whose presence is our true home. We are alienated from God, our true selves, one another, and the creational environment.

Some of the questions that arise when we look at the story of the Scriptures through this theme are these: "How can we be brought home? How can the creation be healed and restored? How can death and decay be overcome?" The gospel answers these questions by telling us that Jesus leaves his own true home (Phil 2:6–7), is born away from his earthly parents' home, wanders without a place to lay his head and without a home (Matt 8:20), and is finally crucified outside the city gate, a sign of his exile and rejection (Heb 13:11–12). He takes our place and experiences the exile—the alienated state—that the human race deserves. He is cast out so we can be brought home. This is summed up in Luke 9:31 (the Greek *exodos* is translated "departure" here)—Jesus' death and resurrection are the ultimate exodus and the ultimate escape from exile. When Jesus rises from the grave, he breaks the power of death and becomes a living foretaste of the new heavens and the new earth that will be our true home. He will reconcile "all things" (Col 1:16–20) and remake the world into the garden city of God (Rev 21:1–8; 22:1–2).[10]

This "home" and our sense of it are hinted at in all of our varying forms of homesickness. And it is this sense of home that steers us clear from any number of false home-goings and idolatries.

RELATED THEMES	
Rest and Sabbath	Sin has left us restless. How can we enter God's rest?
Justice and Shalom	The fabric of the world is broken. How can we restore shalom?
Trinity and Community	We were made for personal and interdependent community with God and his people because we reflect the triune God. How can we become part of this community?

The Covenant and Its Fulfillment

Yahweh reveals himself to be the faithful covenant God. In the covenant relationship, the covenant Lord becomes *our* God, and we become *his* people. A covenant is absolutely binding, and indeed the Lord always does what he says. He is absolutely faithful to his word and promises. In turn, he asks us to also be faithful, to do what *we* say we will do. This poses a problem, for we continually break our word.

Just as the exile/homecoming theme points to our need for the world healer, the Yahweh/covenant theme shows us our need to be saved from our transgressions of the law. This theme raises questions like these: "How can God be *both* faithful and true to his law and word *and* faithful and committed to us? How can God be holy and still love his people? How do the holiness and love of God relate in the covenant?" Isaiah points to a resolution when he speaks of the need for both a covenant Lord and a suffering covenant servant. Jesus takes the curse of the covenant so that the blessing of the covenant could come to us (Gal 3:7 – 14). He fulfills the covenant promise of Genesis 3:15 — he is wounded and yet destroys the work of Satan. Jesus fulfils the Abrahamic covenant as well — he truly is the blessing that comes to all nations. His life as the perfect sacrifice fulfills the Mosaic law (Heb 8 – 10).

So, in response to the great question "Are the covenant blessings of God conditional or unconditional?" — the answer is *yes*. Jesus, as the obedient and faithful covenant servant, absolutely fulfilled the conditions of the covenant through his life and his suffering in our place, making it possible for him, as our faithful covenant Lord, to love us *un*conditionally. At the cross, both the law of God and the love of God were fulfilled and satisfied. In the city of God, there is no more curse (Rev 22:3) because the Passover Lamb of God bore the sins of his people. We will be his people — his bride — and he will be our God (Rev 21:2 – 3). History is consummated in the marriage supper of the Lamb (Rev 19:6 – 9). The ultimate love relationship we were built for will be fulfilled.

RELATED THEMES	
Righteousness and Nakedness	We experience shame and guilt. How can our sins be covered?
Marriage and Faithfulness	We long for true love and closure. How can we find it?
Presence and Sanctuary	We are made to flourish in the presence of God. How can we stand in it?

The Kingdom and Its Coming

As the exile/homecoming theme points to our need for the world healer and the Yahweh/covenant theme shows our need to be saved from our transgressions of the law, the kingdom theme shows us the need for a liberator from slavery. As Romans 1:25 tells us, whatever we worship we serve, and since we all must worship something, we are enslaved to various forces and powers in this world. The search for a true leader, judge, and king absorbs much of the history of God's people (see Deut 17:14–20; 2 Sam 7). None of these leaders fully succeed in protecting the people from falling into idolatry, servitude, and exile. This raises one key question: "How can any king be powerful enough to liberate us from slavery this great?"

The answer announced in the gospel is that God himself must come. Mark 1:1–3 declares that Jesus is the divine King returning to take up his kingdom.[11] The power of Christ's kingly rule is now present among gathered Christians (Luke 17:20–21), liberating people from false masters and enslaving idols. Among the disciples, the kingdom is a new human order in which power, money, recognition, and success are properly reordered in light of the registry of the kingdom. It is not that these things no longer matter but that they become transposed by the unleashing of Christ's new creation—by service, generosity, and humility (Luke 6:17–49). Jesus' kingship is not like human kingships, for it wins influence through suffering service, not coercive power. We enter it not through strength but through the weakness of repentance and the new birth (John 3) and becoming like a child (Matt 18:3–4).

Christ's liberating rule is not fully here. All his disciples are to pray for it to come, according to Matthew 6:10, and at the end of time we will receive it in completion (Matt 25:34). But finally the day comes when the city of God will descend. It contains the throne of God — the seat of the kingdom (Rev 22:3) — from which the renewal of all things proceeds (Rev 21:3–6). This is the ecstatic enthronement depicted in Psalms 96–98. When God returns to rule, even the rivers will clap their hands and the mountains will sing for joy that their liberator has finally come (Ps 98:8; Rom 8:21–22). The freedom and joy of the kingdom of heaven will come to earth.

Although each of these themes emphasizes a unique aspect of the story of the Bible, there is no contradiction — only harmony — among these different ways of communicating the gospel. The Bible's story line tells us at least four things:

1. What God wants for us (Creation)
2. What happened to us and what went wrong with the world (Fall)
3. What God has done in Jesus Christ to put things right (Redemption)
4. How history will turn out in the end as a result (Restoration)

This story can be — and is — told in multiple ways, using multiple themes, since both sin and salvation are multidimensional. This does not mean the gospel cannot be presented simply, nor does it contradict the earlier statement that "the gospel is not everything." All of these ways of presenting the gospel must still emphasize that it is news — an announcement of what God has done and will do.

However, whenever we flesh out the good news, even in a very brief way, we will put it into the context of one or some of these themes, and when we do this, we will shade things a bit toward some aspects of the biblical story and away from others.

RELATED THEMES	
Image and Likeness	Loving God supremely is the only way to truly love anything else and become your true self, to become truly free (2 Cor 4:4; Col 1:15).
Idolatry and Freedom	Serving God supremely is the only way to freedom.
Wisdom and the Word	Submission to the Word of God is the way to wisdom.

The Gospel Must Be Contextualized

The gospel is not a simple thing. We know this because its expression in the themes of the Bible is inexhaustibly deep and rich. But a second reason we know it is that humanity, in both its perfect design and fallen nature, is also complex and varied. The gospel has supernatural versatility to address the particular hopes, fears, and idols of every culture and every person. This points us to the need for contextualization.

In 1 Corinthians 1:22–25, for example, Paul explains that when he spoke to Greeks, he first confronted their culture's idol of speculation and philosophy with the "foolishness" of the cross, and then he presented Christ's salvation as true wisdom. When he spoke to Jews, however, he first confronted their culture's idol of power and accomplishment with the "weakness" of the cross, and then he presented the gospel as true power. One of these gospel forms was tailored to Bible-believing people who thought they would be justified by works on judgment day, while the other was tailored to pagans. These two approaches can also be discerned in Paul's speeches in Acts, some of which were given to Jews and some to pagans. Luke provides three summaries of Paul's gospel preaching.

1. In Acts 13, Paul communicates to Jews and Gentile God-fearers.
2. In Acts 14, Paul addresses noneducated pagans.
3. Acts 17 is a digest of Paul's sermon to philosophers and educated pagans.

It is instructive to see how his audience's capacities and beliefs shape the way Paul presents and argues for the gospel. Different cultural audiences respond to different approaches of nuancing and shaping the same message.

Gospel contextualization is an enormous subject requiring great care, and so the third part of this book is dedicated to it. It is only necessary at this point to observe that one of the reasons the gospel is never given in exactly the same form is not only the diverse richness of the biblical material itself, with all of its intercanonical themes, but the diverse richness of humanity. Paul himself presented the gospel content in different ways — using different orders, arguments, levels of emphasis, and so on — to different cultures. And we should too. The gospel is so rich that it can be communicated in a form that fits every situation. It is a *singular* message, but it is not a *simple* message.

DISCUSSION QUESTIONS

1. Have you or others you know ever felt a pressure to create or adopt a "single, one-size-fits-all gospel presentation that should be used everywhere, that serves as a test of orthodoxy"? What is the appeal of this? What are the risks?

2. Which of the intercanonical themes described in this chapter most resonated with you? Which intercanonical theme would best resonate with non-Christians in your ministry context? With people in your own church? What new ways of communicating the gospel does this open up for you?

3. Read the three passages in Acts cited at the end of the chapter. Jot down a few notes about the differences among Paul's gospel presentations. What does this exercise tell you about your own audience's "capacities and beliefs" and how they should shape the way you present and argue for the gospel?

Chapter 3

THE GOSPEL AFFECTS EVERYTHING

We have seen that *the gospel is not everything*, meaning it must be distinguished as an announcement of news, distinct from its results and implications, and that *the gospel is not a simple thing*, meaning it cannot be packaged in a single standard form. My third contention, that *the gospel affects virtually everything*, builds on these two statements.

In his article "The Gospel of Jesus Christ (1 Corinthians 15:1–19)," D. A. Carson surveys the ethical directives of 1 Corinthians and draws this conclusion:

[This] book ... repeatedly shows how the gospel rightly works out in the massive transformation of attitudes, morals, relationships, and cultural interactions ...

Just as Paul found it necessary to hammer away at the outworking of the gospel in every domain of the lives of the Corinthians, so we must do the same today ...

It does not take much to think through how the gospel must also transform the business practices and priorities of Christians in commerce, the priorities of young men steeped in indecisive but relentless narcissism, the lonely anguish and often the guilty pleasures of single folk who pursue pleasure but who cannot find happiness, the tired despair of those living on the margins, and much more. And this must be done, not by attempting to abstract social principles from the gospel, still less by endless focus on the periphery in a vain effort to sound prophetic, but precisely by preaching and teaching and living out in our churches the glorious gospel of our blessed Redeemer.[1]

Even though the gospel is a set of truths to understand and believe, it cannot *remain* a set of beliefs if it is truly believed and understood. As Lesslie Newbigin writes, "The Christian story provides us with such a set of lenses, not something for us to look *at*, but for us to look *through*."[2] Paul says as much in Romans 12:1, when he looks back on his rich exposition of the doctrine of justification in chapters 1–11: "Therefore, I urge you, brothers and sisters, in view of God's mercy, to offer your bodies as a living sacrifice." Scripture teaches that the gospel creates an entire way of life and affects literally everything about us. It is a power (Rom 1:16–17) that creates new life in us (Col 1:5–6; 1 Pet 1:23–25).

The Richness of the Gospel

New Testament scholar Simon Gathercole offers the following outline of the gospel taught in common by Paul and the Gospel writers:

1. The Son of God emptied himself and came into the world in Jesus Christ, becoming a servant.
2. He died on the cross as a substitutionary sacrifice.
3. He rose from the grave as the firstfruits of a whole renewed world.[3]

Each of these three truths can be fleshed out to show that the implications of the gospel are endless.

The Incarnation and the "Upside-Down" Aspect of the Gospel

Because Jesus was the king who became a servant, we see a reversal of values in his kingdom administration (Luke 6:20–26). In Jesus' kingdom, the poor, sorrowful, and persecuted are above the rich, recognized, and satisfied. The first shall be last (Matt 19:30). Why would this be?

This reversal is a way of imitating the pattern of Christ's salvation (Phil 2:1–11). Though Jesus was rich, he became poor. Though he was a king, he served. Though he was the greatest, he made himself the servant of all. He triumphed over sin not by taking up power but by serving sacrificially. He "won" through losing everything. This is a complete reversal of the world's way of thinking, which values power, recognition, wealth, and status. The gospel, then, creates a new kind of servant community, with people who live out an entirely alternate way of being human. Racial and class superiority, accrual of money and power at the expense of others, yearning for popularity and recognition—all are marks of living in the world. They represent the opposite of the gospel mind-set.

The Atonement and the "Inside-Out" Aspect of the Gospel

The Pharisees tended to emphasize the externals of the covenant—the covenant boundary markers of Sabbath observance, circumcision, Torah, and so on—rather than a regenerated heart (Luke 11:39–41). God's kingdom, however, "is not a matter of eating and drinking, but of righteousness, peace and joy in the Holy Spirit" (Rom 14:17). Why would this be?

Jesus took our place on the cross and accomplished salvation for us, which we receive freely as a gift. Traditional religion teaches that if we do good deeds and follow the moral rules in our external behavior, God will come into our hearts, bless us, and give us salvation. In other words, if I obey, God will love and accept me. But the gospel is the reverse of this: If I know in my heart that God has accepted me and loves me freely by grace, then I can begin to obey, out of inner joy and gratitude. Religion is outside in, but the gospel is inside out. We are justified by grace alone, not by works; we are beautiful and righteous in God's sight by the work of Christ. Once we gain this understanding on the inside, it revolutionizes how we relate to God, to ourselves, and to others on the outside.

The Resurrection and the "Forward-Back" Aspect of the Gospel

Jesus is resurrected, but we are not. He has inaugurated the kingdom of God, but it is not fully present. The coming of the messianic King occurs in two stages. At his first coming, he saved us from the penalty of sin and gave us the presence of the Holy Spirit, the down payment of the age to come (2 Cor 1:21–22; Eph 1:13–14). At the end of time, he will come to complete what he began at the first coming, saving us from the dominion and very presence of sin and evil. He will bring a new creation, a material world cleansed of all brokenness.

Christians now live in light of that future reality. We evangelize, telling people about the gospel and preparing them for the judgment. We also help the poor and work for justice, because we know that this is God's will and that he will ultimately overcome all oppression. We teach Christians to integrate their faith and their work so they can be culture makers, working for human flourishing—the common good. The "already but not yet" of the kingdom keeps us from utopian, triumphalistic visions of cultural takeover on the one hand, and from pessimism or withdrawal from society on the other.

A church that truly understands the implications of the biblical gospel, letting the "message of Christ dwell among [it] richly" (Col 3:16), will look like an unusual hybrid of various church forms and stereotypes. Because of the inside-out, substitutionary atonement aspect, the church will place great emphasis on personal conversion, experiential grace renewal, evangelism, outreach, and church planting. This makes it look like an evangelical-charismatic church. Because of the upside-down, kingdom/incarnation aspect, the church will place great emphasis on deep community, cell groups or house churches, radical giving and sharing of resources, spiritual disciplines, racial reconciliation, and living with the poor. This makes it look like an Anabaptist "peace" church. Because of the forward-back, kingdom/restoration aspect, the church will place great emphasis on seeking the welfare of the city, neighborhood and civic involvement, cultural engagement, and training people to work in "secular" vocations out of a Christian worldview. This makes it look like a mainline church or, perhaps, a Kuyperian Reformed church. Very few churches, denominations, or movements integrate all of these ministries and emphases. Yet I believe that a comprehensive view of the biblical gospel — one that grasps the gospel's inside-out, upside-down, and forward-back aspects — will champion and cultivate them all. This is what we mean by a Center Church.

The Gospel Changes Everything

The gospel is not just the ABCs but the A to Z of the Christian life. It is inaccurate to think the gospel is what saves non-Christians, and then Christians mature by trying hard to live according to biblical principles. It is more accurate to say that we are saved by believing the gospel, and then we are transformed in every part of our minds, hearts, and lives by believing the gospel more and more deeply as life goes on (see Rom 12:1 – 2; Phil 1:6; 3:13 – 14).

In the first chapter, we introduced the idea that there are two errors that constantly seek to steal the gospel from us. On the one hand, "moralism/religion/legalism" stresses truth without grace, for it claims we must obey the truth to be saved. On the other hand, "relativism/irreligion/liberalism" stresses grace without truth, for it claims we are all accepted by God (if there is a God), and we each have to decide what is true for us. We must never forget that Jesus was full of grace *and* truth (John 1:14). "Truth" without grace is not really truth, and "grace" without truth is not really grace. Any religion or philosophy of life that de-emphasizes or loses one or the other of these truths falls into legalism or into license. Either way, the joy and power and "release" of the gospel are stolen — by one thief or the other.

Edward Fisher's *The Marrow of Modern Divinity* is a classic, comprehensive description of how important it is to remember the two enemies of the gospel. Fisher discusses how legalism can be of two types, either of the theological type (a theology that mixes faith and works and is not clear on free justification) or simply of a moralistic spirit and attitude. He also warns of the opposite error of antinomianism, an attitude that is afraid to ever say, "You *ought*," and refrains from insisting that God's law must be obeyed.[4]

The power of the gospel comes in two movements. It first says, "I am more sinful and flawed than I ever dared believe," but then quickly follows with, "I am more accepted and loved than I ever dared hope." The former outflanks antinomianism, while the latter staves off legalism. One of the greatest challenges is to be vigilant in both directions *at once*. Whenever we find ourselves fighting against one of these errors, it is extraordinarily easy to combat it by slipping into the other. Here's a test: if you think one of these errors is much more dangerous than the other, you are probably partially participating in the one you fear less.

Unlike legalism or antinomianism, an authentic grasp of the

gospel of Christ will bring increasing transformation and wholeness across all the dimensions of life that were marred by the fall. By removing the primary cause of all of our alienations—our separation from God—it also treats the alienations that flow from it. The gospel addresses our greatest need and brings change and transformation to every area of life. Let's look at just a few of the ways that the gospel changes us.

Discouragement and depression. When a person is depressed, the moralist says, "You are breaking the rules. Repent." On the other hand, the relativist says, "You just need to love and accept yourself." Absent the gospel, the moralist will work on behavior, and the relativist will work on the emotions—and only superficialities will be addressed instead of the heart. Assuming the depression has no physiological base, the gospel will lead us to examine ourselves and say, "Something in my life has become more important than God—a pseudo-savior, a form of works-righteousness." The gospel leads us to embrace repentance, not to merely set our will against superficialities.

Love and relationships. Moralism often turns relationships into a blame game. This occurs when a moralist is traumatized by severe criticism and in reaction maintains a self-image as a good person by blaming others. Moralism can also cause people to procure love as the way to earn salvation; gaining love convinces them they are worthy persons. This, in turn, often creates codependency—you must save yourself by saving others. On the other hand, much relativism reduces love to a negotiated partnership for mutual benefit. You relate only as long as it does not cost you anything. Without the gospel, the choice is to selfishly use others or to selfishly let yourself be used by others. The gospel leads us to do neither. We selflessly sacrifice and commit, but not out of a need to convince ourselves or others that we are acceptable. We can love a person enough to confront, yet stay with the person even when it does not benefit us.

Sexuality. The moralist tends to see sex as dirty, or at least as a dangerous impulse that leads constantly to sin. The relativist/pragmatist sees sex as merely a biological and physical appetite. The gospel shows us that sexuality is supposed to reflect the self-giving of Christ. He gave himself completely, without conditions. Consequently, we are not to seek intimacy while holding back the rest of our lives. If we give ourselves sexually, we are also to give ourselves legally, socially, and personally. Sex is to be shared only in a totally committed, permanent relationship of marriage.

Family. Moralism can make a person a slave to parental expectations, while relativism/pragmatism sees no need for family loyalty or keeping promises and covenants if they do not meet one's needs. The gospel frees us from making parental approval a form of psychological salvation by pointing to how God is the ultimate Father. Grasping this, we will be neither too dependent nor too hostile toward our parents.

Self-control. Moralists tell us to control our passions out of fear of punishment. This is a volition-based approach. Relativists tell us to express ourselves and find out what is right for us. This is an emotion-based approach. The gospel tells us that the free, unshakable grace of God "teaches us to say 'No'" to our passions (Titus 2:12) if we will only listen to it. It gives us new appetites and affections.[5] The gospel leads us to a whole-person approach that begins with truth descending into the heart.

Race and culture. The moralist/conservative bias is to use truth to evaluate cultures. Feeling superior to others in the impulse of self-justifying pride, moralists idolize their culture as supreme. The relativist/liberal approach is to relativize all cultures ("We can all get along because there is no truth"). The gospel leads us, on the one hand, to be somewhat critical of all cultures, including our own (since truth *is* objective and real). On the other hand, it leads us to recognize we are morally superior to no one, since we are saved by grace alone. In this instance, the gospel is the grand leveler. Both sin and grace strip everyone of every boast. *"All* have sinned" (Rom 3:23, emphasis added); "there is *no one* righteous, not even one" (Rom 3:10, emphasis added; cf. Ps 143:2); therefore, *"whoever* believes in [Jesus] shall not perish but have eternal life" (John 3:16, emphasis added; cf. Mark 16:16; John 3:36; 5:24; 7:38; 11:26). For *in Christ* "there is neither Jew nor Gentile, neither slave nor free, nor is there male and female" (Gal 3:28). Christianity is universal in that it welcomes *everybody*, but it is also particular in its confession that Jesus is Lord, and culture and ethnicity (or whatever other identity) are not. Gospel-relying Christians will exhibit both moral conviction and compassion with flexibility.

Witness. The moralist believes in proselytizing, because "we are right, and they are wrong." Such an approach is almost always offensive. The relativist/pragmatist approach denies the legitimacy of evangelism altogether. Yet the gospel produces a constellation of traits in us. We are compelled to share the gospel out of generosity and love, not guilt. We are freed from the fear of being ridiculed or hurt by others, since we have already received the favor of God by grace. Our dealings with others reflect humility because we know we are saved only by grace alone, not because of our superior insight or character. We are hopeful about everyone, even the "hard cases," because we were saved only because of grace, not because we were people likely to become Christians. We are courteous and careful with people. We don't have to push or coerce them, for it is only God's grace that opens hearts, not our eloquence or persistence or even their openness (Exod 4:10–12). Together, these traits create not only an excellent neighbor in a multicultural society but also a winsome evangelist.

Human authority. Moralists tend to obey human authorities (family, tribe, government, and cultural customs) too anxiously, since they rely heavily on their self-image as upright persons. Relativists/

pragmatists will either obey human authority too much (since they have no higher authority by which they can judge their culture) or else too little (since they may obey only when they know they can't get away with it). The result is either authoritarianism or a disregard for the proper place of authority. The gospel gives a standard by which to oppose human authority (if it contradicts the gospel), as well as an incentive to obey the civil authorities from the heart, even when we could get away with disobedience. To confess Jesus as Lord was simultaneously to confess that Caesar was not. Though there have been several studies of late that discuss the "counter-imperial" tenor of various texts, it is important to stress that the Bible is not so much against governing authorities or "empire" as such but that it prescribes a proper reordering of power. It is not that Jesus usurped the throne of Caesar but that when we allow Caesar to overstep his bounds, he is usurping the throne of Christ and leading people into idolatry.

Guilt and self-image. When someone says, "I can't forgive myself," it indicates that some standard or condition or person is more central to this person's identity than the grace of God. God is the only God who forgives—no other "god" will. If you cannot forgive yourself, it is because you have failed your true god—that is, whatever serves as your real righteousness—and it is holding you captive. The moralists' false god is usually a god of their imagination, a god that is holy and demanding but not gracious. The relativist/pragmatist's false god is usually some achievement or relationship.

This is illustrated by the scene in the movie *The Mission* in which Rodrigo Mendoza, the former slave-trading mercenary played by Robert de Niro, converts to the church and as a way of showing penance drags his armor and weapons up steep cliffs. In the end, however, he picks up his armor and weapons to fight against the colonialists and dies at their hand. His picking up his weapons demonstrates he never truly converted from his mercenary ways, just as his penance demonstrated he didn't get the message of forgiveness in the first place. The gospel brings rest and assurance to our consciences because Jesus shed his blood as a "ransom" for our sin (Mark 10:45). Our reconciliation with God is not a matter of keeping the law to earn our salvation, nor of berating ourselves when we fail to keep it. It is "the gift of God" (Rom 6:23).

Without the gospel, our self-image is based on living up to some standards — either our own or someone else's imposed on us. If we live up to those standards, we will be confident but not humble; if we don't live up to them, we will be humble but not confident. Only in the gospel can we be both enormously bold and utterly sensitive and humble, for we are *simul justus et peccator*, both perfect and sinner!

Joy and humor. Moralism eats away at real joy and humor because the system of legalism forces us to take our self (our image, our appearance, our reputation) *very* seriously. Relativism/pragmatism, on the other hand, tends toward pessimism as life goes on because of the inevitable cynicism that grows from a lack of hope for the world ("In the end, evil will triumph because there is no judgment or divine justice"). If we are saved by grace alone, this salvation is a constant source of amazed delight. Nothing is mundane or matter-of-fact about our lives. It is a miracle we are Christians, and the gospel, which creates bold humility, should give us a far deeper sense of humor and joy. We don't have to take ourselves seriously, and we are full of hope for the world.

Attitudes toward class. Moralists, when they look at the poor, tend to see their entire plight stemming from a lack of personal responsibility. As a result, they scorn the poor as failures. Relativists tend to underemphasize the role of personal responsibility and see the poor as helpless victims needing the experts to save them. The poor themselves either feel like failures or angrily blame their problems on others.

The gospel, however, leads us to be humble, free from moral

superiority, because we know we were spiritually bankrupt yet saved by Christ's free generosity. It leads us to be gracious, not worried too much about people getting what they deserve because we are aware that *none* of us deserve the grace of Christ. It also inclines us to be respectful of poor Christian believers as our brothers and sisters in Christ, people from whom we can learn. The gospel alone can produce a humble respect for and solidarity with the poor (see Pss 140:12; 146:9; Prov 14:31; 21:13; 22:22–23; 29:7).

In James 1:9–10, the poor Christian "ought to take pride in their high position" but the rich Christian "should take pride in their humiliation — since they will pass away like a wild flower." Here James is using the gospel on his listeners' class-consciousness. Everyone in Christ is at the same time a sinner who deserves death and also an adopted child of God, fully accepted and loved. But James proposes that the well-off believer would spiritually benefit by thinking about his or her sinfulness before God, since out in the world he or she gets a lot of acclaim. The poor believer, however, would spiritually benefit by thinking about his or her new high spiritual status, since out in the world he or she gets nothing but disdain.

In a remarkable, similar move, Paul tells the Christian slave owner Philemon that his slave, Onesimus, must be treated as "a fellow man and as a brother in the Lord" (Phlm 16). Therefore, Paul says, he should welcome and treat his slave "as you would welcome me" (v. 17). By teaching that Christians who understand the gospel should have a radically different way of understanding and wielding power, Paul deeply undermines the very institution of slavery. When both master and slave recognize each other as sinners saved by grace and beloved siblings, "slavery has been abolished even if its outer institutional shell remains." The gospel "emptied [slavery] of its inner content."[6]

● ● ●

Most of our problems in life come from a lack of proper orientation to the gospel. Pathologies in the church and sinful patterns in our individual lives ultimately stem from a failure to think through the deep implications of the gospel and to grasp and believe the gospel through and through. Put positively, the gospel transforms our hearts and our thinking and changes our approaches to absolutely everything. When the gospel is expounded and applied in its fullness in any church, that church will look unique. People will find in it an attractive, electrifying balance of moral conviction and compassion.

D. A. Carson writes the following:

> The gospel is regularly presented not only as truth to be received and believed, but the very power of God to transform (see 1 Cor 2; 1 Thess 2:4; [Rom 1:16–17]) ...
>
> One of the most urgently needed things today is a careful treatment of how the gospel, biblically and richly understood, ought to shape everything we do in the local church, all of our ethics, all of our priorities.[7]

But how does this happen? What does a church that believes in the centrality of the gospel actually look like? How does a church, or even a group of churches, change to become a gospel-centered community of faith? There must first be a life-changing recovery of the gospel—a revival in the life of the church and in the hearts of individuals. We call this *gospel renewal.*

DISCUSSION QUESTIONS

1. Keller writes, "Here's a test: if you think one of these errors [legalism or license] is much more dangerous than the other, you are probably partially participating in the one you fear less." Which error have you tended to fear less, and why?

2. Keller writes, "The primary cause of all of our alienations [is] our separation from God." How has the gospel mended this primary ailment in you and how has it helped curb the many other symptoms that flow from it? How does this experience prepare you to minister to alienated people?

3. Keller writes, "The gospel addresses our greatest need and brings change and transformation to every area of life." The gospel also treats the alienations that flow from our alienation from God. Rehearse, in your own words, how the gospel treats at least three of the following areas:

   - discouragement and depression
   - love and relationships
   - sexuality
   - family and parental expectations
   - self-control
   - racial and cultural differences
   - our motive for witness
   - obedience to human authority
   - guilt and self-image
   - joy and humor
   - our attitudes toward class

4. Look at the three aspects of the gospel dealt with in this chapter: incarnation/upside-down, atonement/inside-out, and resurrection/forward-back. Compare these to the similar outline in the section titled "The Gospel Has Chapters" in chapter 1 (p. 36). How can you sharpen and clarify the way you set the gospel within the story line of the Bible?

REFLECTIONS ON GOSPEL THEOLOGY

Michael Horton, professor of theology and apologetics at Westminster Seminary, California

On several occasions over the years, I've taken friends and family to Redeemer Presbyterian Church for the Sunday morning service. I brought them there because I knew they would hear God's lordly claim over their lives and his gracious gospel—and they did. So I'm grateful for the invitation to enter into conversation with Tim Keller about *Center Church*, especially at the point where I am most grateful for his ministry, namely, his clear proclamation of the gospel.

"*The gospel is not everything,*" Keller writes, but "*the gospel affects virtually everything*" (p. 61). This should become a common phrase among us, and it is the central claim of these first few chapters of his book.

The Gospel Is Not Everything

The starting point for Tim Keller is the marvelous simplicity of the good news, citing J. I. Packer's terse summary: "God saves sinners." As Packer observes, each word can be unpacked in volumes. As someone has said, the gospel is so accessible that anyone can wade in it and so profound that one can swim in its depths without ever touching the bottom. At the outset, Keller helpfully defines the gospel as a specific announcement of God's saving work in Jesus Christ.

It is a proclamation, news of a rescue operation—specifically, being "rescued from the 'coming wrath' at the end of history (1 Thess 1:10)." Ever since the fall, our history lies under the curse of sin and death. We can see evidence of this on the horizontal level: relationships between human beings, for example. Yet the root of this mess is the rupture in "our 'vertical' relationship with God" (p. 29).

As their name suggests, evangelicals have sought to define the gospel clearly. In recent years especially, there have been myriad attempts to nail down the most precise summary. Many of us were reared on a simple formula like the Four Spiritual Laws, but there has been a growing sense that a wider and deeper lens is needed. It's not only news of God's grace toward individuals, but a sweeping announcement of cosmic redemption. Therefore, the gospel is not just the message of Christ's substitutionary death for our sins and resurrection for our justification and new birth. The gospel necessarily includes Christ's incarnation and life, as well as his ascension, the giving of the Spirit at Pentecost, and his eventual return. This more inclusive view of Christ's saving actions is consistent with Scripture and the best preaching throughout church history. Some overreact in emphasizing this more inclusive view of the gospel by downplaying the unmistakably scriptural emphasis on Christ's judicial work in favor of various alternative "centers" in the biblical witness to salvation in Christ. Wisely, Keller exhorts us to include all of these aspects without displacing Christ's vicarious substitution at the heart of the gospel.

I found especially helpful Keller's concern to distinguish the gospel from its effects. As he states, these two are "neither confused nor separated." When it comes to words like *redeem*, *reconcile*, and *liberate*, there has been a shift in recent years away from the aorist tense, with God as the subject of the action, to the present tense, where we ourselves are the subject. Instead of God having reconciled the world to himself in Christ, having redeemed and liberated sinners from death and the condemnation and tyranny of sin, we are invited to participate in (even to be!) his ongoing incarnation and saving work in the world. In addition to being ministers of reconciliation by proclaiming the gospel, we are told that we *are* the agents of reconciliation.

So I sympathize with Keller when he relates his own experience: "I have often heard people preach this way: 'The good news is that God *is* healing and *will* heal the world of all its hurts; therefore, the work of the gospel is to work for justice and peace in the world'" (p. 31). This mistakes effects for causes. As Keller reminds us, "It confuses what the gospel *is* with what the gospel *does*" (p. 31). That said, we should acknowledge that the gospel is not only about what God has accomplished for us in the past; it is also about what he promises us in the future. "The *future* is ours because of Christ's work finished in the *past*" (p. 31). The key to maintaining the biblical gospel is seeing the triune God as the subject of this saving action. The gospel isn't doing something or joining something, but "*receiving* something [Christ's finished work]" (p. 31). The gospel is "news that creates a life of love, but the life of love is not itself the gospel" (p. 32). Appealing to D. A. Carson's study of *euangelion*, Keller reminds us that the gospel is something to be proclaimed, not something for us to do or complete (pp. 27–28).

Drawing on J. Gresham Machen's distinction between the gospel and "presuppositions" of the gospel (p. 33), Keller then helpfully shows us that while the gospel itself centers on Christ's redeeming work, it cannot be understood properly apart from the Trinity, the incarnation, and original sin. (I would also include the incarnation in the gospel, as Keller does later.) "In other words, we must *not* just preach the Bible in general; we must preach the gospel. Yet unless those listening to the message understand the Bible in general, they won't grasp the gospel" (p. 33). "In light of the biblical usage, then, we should observe that [the gospel's] chapters 1 (God and Creation),

2 (Fall and Sin), and 4 (Faith) are not, strictly speaking, 'the gospel.' They are prologue and epilogue" (p. 36).

All of this points us to the usefulness of the classic distinction between the gospel in its *broader* and *narrower* sense. Keller wants to affirm the narrower sense—the gospel as a specific announcement of God's rescue operation in Christ—without losing sight of the broader definition of the gospel as including all of God's saving promises that are "Yes" and "Amen" in Christ (2 Cor 1:20).

As the gospel's chapter titles indicate, Keller's primary concern in this section is to curb the tendency in our day to lose the gospel's clear center while still retaining its relevance for every aspect of doctrine, worship, and life. Evangelicals have an unhealthy tendency to make everything "the gospel." Viewed positively, this can concentrate the church's focus for theology and mission in keeping with our Lord's Great Commission (Matt 28:19–20). Yet this tendency can also reduce to relative unimportance many things that are admittedly not "the gospel." It can lead us to confuse the gospel with other things—many of them good and even biblical—that are *not* the gospel.

We see the first problem—the dismissal of non-gospel differences—whenever someone shrugs over a disagreement and says, "It's not a gospel issue." Evangelicals make the mistake of including truths that are not part of the gospel itself among their core "gospel" issues, and then excluding issues that are, in fact, part of the biblical gospel. Christ's commission is to preach the gospel, baptize, and teach hearers to obey everything he has commanded—in both doctrine and life (Matt 28:20). We need to remember that Christ is Lord of all, not just Lord of what we personally consider to be gospel issues. Whatever is taught in Scripture, whether in doctrine or practice, is to be taught and followed by his church.

We also make a mistake when we think that *everything* is the gospel. When everything is about the gospel, it's easy to forget the gospel itself, the uniqueness of the message. "Faith comes from hearing the message, and the message is heard through the word about Christ" (Rom 10:17). As stated earlier, the gospel is something we hear, not something we do. We are to live in a way that *commends* the gospel. The gospel *changes* our lives, and that change should be a fragrance of life to those whom the Spirit is calling through the gospel (2 Cor 2:15), but the gospel itself is a story about God and his redeeming, reconciling, and restoring work in Christ. The gospel frees us to obey God's law in the power of the Spirit as forgiven, justified, adopted sinners who are being conformed to the image of God's Son. Our agenda, as disciples of Christ, is bigger than just "the gospel."

Keller maintains balance here and avoids swinging to either extreme. As he says, the gospel *affects* everything (see chapter 3). I was reminded of what he means the other day when my daughter and I were watching a beautiful sunset casting a spectrum of amber and scarlet on the clouds. "Jesus made that," she said. *Yes*, I thought to myself, *but the Father and the Spirit were in on the act as well.* Still my daughter was recognizing that her mediator in salvation is also the mediator she meets in creation and providence. To be genuinely evangelical is to let the gospel soak in this way—not only to motivate our agendas but to shape them as well.

Let me give you another example. As ministers, the gospel should affect how we think about our ministry and how we serve others. We should see those whom we serve not as consumers or as burdens, but as images of God and fellow brothers and sisters with us in a redeemed family. We may need to rethink our church's ministry from the ground up, do a little spring cleaning, and trim the distractions away so we can more faithfully distribute Christ and his gifts for "you and your children and for all who are far off—for all whom the Lord our God will call" (Acts 2:39).

Integrating Individual and Cosmic Aspects

After distinguishing (without separating) the gospel itself from its effects, Keller seeks to integrate the individual and cosmic import of salvation. "How can I be put right with God?" is a biblical question, and there is no faithful preaching of the gospel that ignores it. Yet we also need to ask a broader question: "What hope is there for the world?" Here, Keller draws our focus to the relationship between propositions (doctrinal statements) and the plotline of "creation, fall, redemption, and restoration" (p. 34). Martin Luther's question, "How can I find a gracious God?" is marginalized by those who focus on the gospel as something more like, quoting J. I. Packer, "God's plan to bless Israel, and through Israel the world, came to its climax in and through Christ" (p. 35). I appreciate the point Keller draws here from Simon Gathercole, who says that according to the New Testament, the gospel encompasses three foci: "the identity of Jesus as Son of God and Messiah, the death of Jesus for sin and justification, and the establishment of the reign of God and the new creation" (p. 36). This is a helpful summary of what the gospel covers.

Yet here is also my first area of disagreement with Keller. I'm not quite as persuaded by his statement that "the narrative approach poses the questions, and the propositional approach supplies the answers" (pp. 35–36). In Scripture, we find that doctrinal propositions arise out of the narrative itself. I do not think we should try to distinguish between the narrative and propositional by reducing them to questions and answers, as Keller suggests. What Keller wishes to overcome is a reductionism that creates a false choice between the *personal* and *global* implications of the gospel. These are the emphases, rather than the categories of *narrative* and *propositional*, that seem more determinative to me. "How can I find a gracious God?" can be answered narratively or in a series of bullet points. Writers like N. T. Wright summarize their alternative vision in simple propositional statements as well.

To what, then, is the gospel the answer? Sin, which is both condemnation and corruption. Keller points out that sin manifests itself as slavery. "Everyone has to live for something, and if that something is not God, then we are driven by that thing we live for—by overwork to achieve it, by inordinate fear if it is threatened, deep anger if it is being blocked, and inconsolable despair if it is lost" (p. 38). Then Keller points out that the sinful condition brings condemnation. "We all owe a debt that must be paid" (p. 39). This slavery, corruption, and indebtedness can be overcome only by Christ's incarnation, substitution, and restoration (pp. 39–41). Keller reminds us that faith is not the gospel; faith is the way we are set right with God—how we are justified. Once again we're prone to treat faith as our "little work" that somehow earns God's favor, but Keller reminds us that it's "not the quality of the faith itself that saves us," but the object (p. 42). Strictly speaking, we are saved *by Christ*—not *by faith*, but *through faith* in Christ.

The Gospel Is a Simple Thing

As the years wear on, Keller observes, it's easy for churches to want to "go deeper" into advanced doctrinal, spiritual, communal, or therapeutic intrigues (p. 43). The danger, though, is a subtle (or not so subtle) drift from the gospel as the center. "Every form of ministry is empowered by the gospel, based on the gospel, and is a result of the gospel" (p. 43). One of the most illuminating lines in part 1 of *Shaped by the Gospel* is this: "Because the gospel is endlessly rich, it can handle the burden of being the one 'main thing' of a church" (p. 44). However, "if an element of ministry is not recognized as a *result* of the gospel, it may sometimes be mistaken *for* the gospel and eventually supplant the gospel in the church's preaching and teaching" (p. 44).

At the same time, Keller reminds us that while the gospel is a very specific announcement, it is richly complex. When Paul reminded the Corinthians that he had preached nothing other than "Christ crucified" while he was among them, it is unlikely that the apostle simply repeated "Christ crucified" as a slogan. Rather, he saw all roads leading to and from the good news of God's rescue operation in Christ, and he wouldn't allow anything—even good things—to pull him off point. Similarly, as Keller goes on to say in chapter 2, although the gospel can be *presented* simply and even very briefly" (p. 47), it is so multifaceted that we cannot reduce it to a single slogan.

We see the wisdom and relevance of Keller's argument when we consider that among evangelical scholars, there is often a temptation to pit "the kingdom" against "personal salvation" or the Gospels against Paul. Here Keller helpfully points out how all of these diverse canonical voices point to the same evangelical reality. "At the heart of all of the biblical writers' theology is redemption through substitution" (p. 49).

Keller also seeks to reconcile the systematic-theological method (STM) with the redemptive-historical method (RHM). Here I think he is on better footing than he was with his earlier propositional-narrative distinction. "There is no ultimate reason these two approaches should contradict one another ... I would go even further and warn that failing to use both approaches invites danger. The STM, carried out in isolation from the RHM, can produce a Christianity that is rationalistic, legalistic, and individualistic. Similarly, the RHM, carried out in isolation from the STM, tends to produce a Christianity that loves narrative and community but shies away from sharp distinctions between grace and law and between truth and heresy. One approach that draws from both the story line and the themes of Scripture is to read the Bible through *intercanonical themes*" (pp. 50–51).

For me, this section on tying the gospel to the themes of the Bible (pp. 49–57) is the highlight of Keller's three chapters on gospel theology. It's a section I plan to turn to for my own preaching. Keller helpfully shows how to do what he is saying, how to integrate the gospel with the rest of Scripture. "A person can explain the gospel from beginning to end through any of these themes, but no single theme gives the full picture" (p. 51). In particular, I think his example of the "Exile and Our Homecoming" provides a great example of what he is talking about (pp. 52–53). "Exile and Homecoming" is a motif that recurs throughout Scripture. "The Covenant and Its Fulfillment" is another terrific instance of how an integrated approach plays out in the pulpit (pp. 53–55). "All of these ways of presenting the gospel must still emphasize that it is news — an announcement of what God has done and will do" (p. 56).

At the same time, Keller's point that no single theme gives us the full picture is crucial. In the circles to which we each belong, redemptive-historical preaching can become as predictable as topical or doctrinal preaching. It can go something like this: "Here is what God requires and how so-and-so failed, but Christ fulfilled it for us and he is the true X." Motifs can be recycled as easily as the doctrines we love the most. And there is always the temptation to preach the same sermon, regardless of the particular passage. That can happen with themes of "Exile and Homecoming" or "The Covenant and Its Fulfillment" of course. We naturally gravitate toward the motif that strikes us most profoundly, but Keller wisely urges us to resist this temptation to reductionism. Preaching needs to explore the varied facets of the gospel, as well as the exhortations and commands, the doctrines and the narratives, the plotline and the systematic connections. We need not worry we'll run out of material!

Next Keller focuses our attention on contextualizing the gospel (pp. 57–58). Here is another area where we have some disagreement. Keller begins by pointing out that different audiences and contexts hear God's Word differently. To the Greeks, the gospel was "fool-ishness," while to the Jews it was a "stumbling block" (1 Cor 1:23). Paul's preaching in Acts 13 (to a Jewish audience) differs significantly from Acts 17 (to Athenian philosophers). To both he preached the gospel, but with quite different approaches. Keller points out that "contextualization" can become an excuse for *accommodation*, yet it can also be a point of *confrontation*.

Personally, I tend to think that much of the contextualization talk in our day is overinflated. I'm sure that part of my skepticism is due to some forms of contextualization I have encountered in which knowing one's audience becomes more important than knowing God's Word. Yet I'm aware of the opposite danger as well—of preaching sermons from nowhere to no one. If we are to move people from *x* to *y*, we clearly need to know both of those coordinates. Does God's Word transcend time and place? Yes and no. Yes, it comes to us from above, from God, to all contexts throughout all of history. Abraham believed the gospel, just as we do. But the answer is also no. Abraham did not know Christ's person and work to the extent we know it. Although it comes from God ultimately, this Word is delivered through ordinary people called to an extraordinary ministry as prophets and apostles, over many centuries. Their fingerprints are all over the Bible, revealing the peculiar styles, cultural distinctives, and personal emphases of each human writer.

So what does this mean for us now, long after the canon has been completed? We still need to know where we are and especially how our neighbors hear us saying things. We may say things we never intended to communicate, simply because of changing assumptions, language, and social conditioning. At the same time, I don't believe we change *that much* when it comes to the questions and issues the Bible addresses. I also wonder that if we focus too much on the uniqueness of a particular context (generational, political, socio-economic, ethnic, and the like), we fall into the trap of becoming armchair cultural analysts. This can sometimes lead to a church that reflects the pastor's own socialization.

We need to remember that our ultimate location is "in Christ," not in whatever market demographic we've been assigned by the culture. "In Christ," the writings of an ancient bishop in North Africa can be more contemporary and relevant to a believer living today in Los Angeles than the latest rap song, novel, or movie. Part of our job as preachers is to move people from what they *think* is their defining identity (in their culture and time) to their identity in the body of Christ. In other words, God's story is a lot richer, larger, and more comprehensive than any of the others we tell.

In fairness to Tim Keller, his ministry clearly puts content over context. In fact, for him, this is a false antithesis. After all, we are trying to reach *people* with the *gospel*. So when Keller talks "context," I'm all ears. I recall when he came to Westminster Seminary California several years ago and encouraged future pastors to subscribe to the newspapers and magazines their members are most likely to read. Obviously there's some overlap. New Yorkers don't just read *The New Yorker* and folks in Indiana don't just read the *Farmers' Almanac*—many of us read the same things. But there will always need to be some sensitivity to local context. We're all inveterate idolaters, yet we tend to manifest this idolatry in different ways. The gospel is rich and complex enough to liberate us from all of our idols. It's "not only the diverse richness of the biblical material itself," Keller adds, "but the diverse richness of humanity" that leads to different ways of presenting the gospel. "It is a *singular* message, but it is not a *simple* message" (p. 58).

At this point, I'm reminded of Augustine's conversion. As with many others, Paul's letter to the Romans played a key role in Augustine's conversion to Christ, yet it wasn't the typical passages we might think of at first. The passage was Romans 13:12–14:

The night is nearly over; the day is almost here. So let us put aside the deeds of darkness and put on the armor of light. Let us behave decently, as in the daytime, not in carousing and drunkenness, not in sexual immorality and debauchery, not in dissension and jealousy. Rather, clothe yourselves with the Lord Jesus Christ, and do not think about how to gratify the desires of the flesh.

The announcement of our release from the tyranny of sin—specifically, immorality—is part of the gospel, and it was this that caught Augustine's attention. Of course, Augustine became the champion of other facets of the gospel as well—over against the moralism of Pelagius. Yet up to this moment in his life, he had given himself over to the immoral lifestyle described by Paul. To "clothe [himself] with the Lord Jesus Christ" was the strangest—and most liberating—thing he had ever heard. That word needed to be personally contextualized for him. For others, the portal to new life might be a different facet of the diamond: "Therefore, there is now no condemnation for those who are in Christ Jesus" (Rom 8:1) or "the creation itself will be liberated from its bondage to decay and brought into the freedom and glory of the children of God" (8:21). My point is this: It takes a big gospel to announce a big redemption.

Where Is the Law?

Let me state upfront that I have no interest in downplaying the central role of the gospel. As I said earlier, I couldn't agree more with Keller that the gospel affects everything. Still, at points I wondered if something else was missing. What does Keller have to say about that other part of God's speech—namely, God's law?

We should recall that the Great Commission calls the church not only to preach the gospel but also to baptize and to teach

each new follower to obey everything Jesus commanded (Matt 28:19–20). Keller has helpfully reminded us that, while the gospel isn't everything, we can only understand the gospel in the context of the whole teaching of Scripture. The Trinity, creation, the fall, and other important doctrines are crucial underpinnings and presuppositions of the gospel. This is such a helpful way of putting things, but I was left wondering why there weren't more examples of how this plays out in preaching. For example, Keller quotes D. A. Carson's statement, "It does not take much to think through how the gospel must also transform business practices and priorities of Christians in commerce" (p. 61). The gospel gives us an entirely different set of assumptions, convictions, and coordinates, and I can imagine some examples of how that gospel lens could change my view of other people. Still, it would seem that it is largely biblical exhortations—commands—that I would turn to if I wish to identify in concrete terms what the transformed business practices and priorities of Christians in commerce might look like. Even there, I'm still going to have to rely on general revelation quite a bit. For example, there may be some "best practices" that do not come directly from Scripture but that do reflect wise and just dealings between people.

Keller follows this with examples of how the gospel changes everything: our approaches to sexuality, class, self-image, depression, and so forth. Everything he says along those lines is spot-on, and I agree when he writes, "The gospel shows us that sexuality is supposed to reflect the self-giving of Christ. He gave himself completely, without conditions. Consequently, we are not to seek intimacy while holding back the rest of our lives" (p. 68). "Most of our problems in life come from a lack of proper orientation to the gospel" (p. 73). So in the big picture, I couldn't agree more. "Still," I wonder, "what about the 'presuppositions of the gospel,' as well as the law?" The gospel indeed changes our attitudes toward sexuality, but without a solid understanding of creation—affirmation of the natural condition before the fall—part of the gospel's relevance to this issue may be lost. This is especially true in our culture today, where it is simply assumed that individual choice rather than nature determines human identity. While many of our most important problems in life come from a lack of proper orientation to the gospel, I am wary of giving folks the impression that every rough patch in their lives can be solved simply by a better grasp of the gospel. My point is simply that the complex nature of human beings and the sinful condition that Keller highlights elsewhere should be kept in mind at this point.

I wonder if, in the end, it is better to let the gospel do its work without too many specifics from us about the effects it is supposed to have. To be clear, here is what I have in mind: A person struggling with loneliness might be driven to even greater despair by living with the expectation that his problem needs to be solved by the gospel. The fact is that some people are just plain lonely. For whatever reason, perhaps they haven't found a mate. Or perhaps something in their past makes finding intimacy and friendship difficult. The gospel certainly is the anchor in that storm, but it's an anchor despite their experience. Even when depression is not diagnosed as clinical, some people naturally gravitate toward depression. Sinners and sinned against, their experience of living in a fallen world is complex. Keller makes this point more clearly elsewhere in *Center Church*, and he exhibits it in his preaching. All of us struggle with different things, and we all struggle differently with similar things. How does someone respond to the most important news he or she could hear? Many will be overwhelmed—at least over time—by the gospel at just the points Keller mentions. Others won't, even though they believe the same message. Just as we'll go to our grave fighting besetting sins, many, many believers will die feeling lonely, depressed, and lacking a proper sense of themselves—despite their faith in Christ and his gospel.

My point is that we may also need some good "law work" on issues like racism, socioeconomic pride, and other forms of group narcissism. "The power of the gospel comes in two movements," Keller says. "It first says, 'I am more sinful and flawed than I ever dared believe,' but then quickly follows with, 'I am more accepted and loved than I ever dared hope.' The former outflanks antinomianism, while the latter staves off legalism" (p. 66). But shouldn't we say that it is the *law* that handles that first movement, not the gospel? Keller rightly emphasizes that idolatry is the common denominator of these sins. Yet the first work that needs to be done here is a penetrating and soul-searching "first use" of the law—to expose our sin and show our need for Christ. The law reveals our idolatry, and the gospel proclaims freedom from its condemnation and power. The gospel *needs* the law to do its job. And if the gospel delivers us, how does the "third use" of the law direct us—the law as our guide to holiness, to living the Christian life? How does this use of the law "preach" without falling back into legalism? These are perennial questions that pastors are asking, and I believe on this point Tim Keller could offer helpful counsel by clarifying what he means on the relationship between the law and the gospel.

● ● ○

Tim Keller is a model of a pastor-scholar. He has been around long enough to have seen myriad emphases come and go among biblical scholars and theologians. He is also a brilliant synthesizer, which comes through in his analysis of the gospel. It is a pleasure to be brought back again—and again—to the gospel as the center of the church's existence, growth, and mission. Start here—at the center—and even differences here or there on other points are given their proper sense of proportion. Start anywhere else, and even agreements seem trivial.

RESPONSE TO
MICHAEL HORTON

Timothy Keller

Grateful

Michael Horton's essay is full of kind confirmations and appreciations for the main lines of presentation in "Gospel Theology." For this I am grateful, because Michael Horton is certainly one of the premier voices in orthodox Reformed theology today, as his landmark series of systematic theological studies attests. And his agreements are not surprising, since he and I both inhabit that (not terribly large) part of the theological world that wants to clearly distinguish law from gospel but at the same time to see a central and abiding place for the law of God in the life of the Christian.

This is why he can happily affirm the distinction of the gospel itself from the presuppositions of the gospel (doctrines of the Trinity, original sin), as well as from the effects of the gospel (working for justice, loving our neighbor). This keeps us from a creeping doctrinalism, which implies we need to believe the whole of systematic theology to be saved, and legalism, which implies that good deeds in the world are part of the gospel.

Helpful

Horton criticizes me for describing the "narrative" presentation of the gospel (creation-fall-redemption-restoration) over against the propositional approach (God-sin-cross-faith) in too mutually exclusive a way. I claim that the narrative approach mainly raises questions that the propositional formulation can answer. He contends that the two approaches are "emphases" rather than strict "categories" or forms. For example, he argues that it is possible to answer a question like "How can I find a gracious God?" by using narrative, and it is possible to present the plotline of the Bible as a set of bullet points (p. 80). I think his critique hits home. He gives me credit for later seeing the ultimate compatibility of biblical theology and systematic theology, but he thinks that at some points I drive too much of a wedge between the propositional and the narratival. I think he's right.

In light of this admitted misstep, it was instructive to hear Horton's strong praise for my section on how to preach the gospel from intercanonical themes, such as exile, covenant, and kingdom. There, as he points out, I fully integrate the topical-doctrinal and redemptive-historical in preaching the gospel. When I reflected on this, I realized that I am primarily a working preacher, not a teacher of theology, and therefore I am better at showing people what to do than describing how to do it. This doesn't mean we preachers should not write books of theological reflection on what we do. It does mean, I think, that to do ministry well, we need the confluence of voices and perspectives. Many of those writing response essays in this book and the other two books in the series are also not working preachers or, in some cases, ordained ministers. But we need them all.

There is another place of "some disagreement" with Horton that I nevertheless need to place in this category of "helpful." While my main treatment of contextualization comes in a different section of

Center Church, I touch on it in Gospel Theology as well, and that gives Horton an opportunity to state, "Personally, I tend to think that much of the contextualization talk in our day is overinflated" (p. 84). He does not in any way resist the argument that Paul adapted his message to diverse audiences. Nor does he deny the great danger of "preaching sermons from nowhere to no one" (a helpful phrase). The key word here is that his resistance to my emphasis comes from experience he has had "personally." I have heard from others who, like Horton, do not disagree with any of the particulars of my case and description of contextualization, but their personal experience is that the greater danger is young preachers in the church making "knowing one's audience ... more important than knowing God's Word" (p. 84).

I don't question that this is true to a significant degree, though it may depend on where you are looking. In many places there are young ministers putting more time and effort into finding cultural references than into clear presentation of biblical content. I also see the phenomenon of "armchair cultural analysts" who lecture their congregations on the culture instead of using their understanding of culture (without talking about it all the time) to show people the particular ways their hearts resist the claims of the Bible.

However, I too am influenced by where I am looking. In the centers of the greatest global cities in the world, where listeners are highly skeptical secularists or adherents of other religions, I see preachers struggling (and often failing) to communicate the Christian faith in a way that will bring the hearers up short by making them reexamine their own biases and assumptions. Unless you know and understand these background beliefs, I don't see how you can challenge them or call people to repent. A traditional Asian family in a poor part of their Chinese city will find biblical faith offensive at different points from a young, single professional in Paris. Horton is right that the ultimate reason for resistance to the gospel—the sinful rebellion of the human heart—is the same across all times and places. And pride is pride is pride (anywhere), as are guilt and fear and anger. But the form of that rebellion is always culturally shaped. So preachers don't just need to demonstrate cultural sophistication (as so many young ministers try to do). They need to use what they know about the culture, generally without talking directly about it, to bring about conviction of sin.

Still, Horton's caution here helps me. I doubt that my own vantage point is sufficient to grasp the wider situation. "Contextualization" is evidently being used as a banner to justify attitudes that are not healthy rather than as a strategy for persuasion and conviction. When this subject is discussed and taught, those wrong attitudes need to be described and distinguished from the work of contextualizing the gospel.

Intriguing

One of Horton's most important criticisms to reflect on is that some of my rhetoric may be "giving folks the impression that every rough patch in their lives can be solved simply by a better grasp of the gospel" (p. 88). The example he uses is of someone who is lonely for reasons beyond their control. While conceding that "the gospel is the anchor in that storm," he fears that the preaching I encourage might drive the lonely person to despair by the implication that if he or she believed the gospel sufficiently, the pain of loneliness would be completely lifted. He hastens to add that in my actual preaching I avoid that impression but that the strength of my statements elsewhere might lead other preachers to be that simplistic.

If Horton thinks that the presentation of Gospel Theology here leads to that impression (and I'm not sure he is saying that), I don't agree. The remedy for this kind of preaching should be found in the earlier part of the Gospel Theology section, where it is said that the gospel must be preached through the great narrative biblical themes. One of those themes is the "already but not yet" of the kingdom. The only way to give listeners the impression that the gospel will solve your problems (i.e., remove all the pain of loneliness) is to avoid explaining or expounding on this biblical theme.

Indeed, real expository preaching can't possibly leave the impression that Horton is rightly concerned about. Psalm 88 is a powerful psalm by a lonely man who has lost both friend and neighbor so now darkness is the only friend he has left (v. 18). The psalm is one of the few that ends without a note of hope in God. The inescapable conclusion is that loneliness does not have an easy solution. It can last a long time. The very form and existence of the psalm, however, testify to God's empathy and grace, two things that come to their ultimate expression in the incarnation and the cross. This is the grace that brings us through our own darkest times. Now, when you preach the gospel like that—and I don't see how you cannot if you preach expositorily—no one should think that "the gospel is the answer to your problems" means "the gospel solves and removes your problem."

Having said that, I view this critique as helpful. I can see in the church at large exactly what Horton sees—that many people do indeed preach the gospel in this reductionistic way. There are some so galvanized by the message of free grace that they grab it and run with it, ignoring all the nuances and balances, and flatten the preaching of it to simply "if you really believe hard enough that you are accepted, then all of your problems will be solved." In correcting them, however, we must not obscure what Horton calls "the gospel as the anchor" factor, namely, that the gospel is the main resource for facing every problem. Without the platform of knowing I am "in Christ," there is no way to handle losses, because the things we are losing will have an inordinate hold on us. Also, while the gospel is not the only instrument we use to face our problems (we also use

Christian relationships, disciplines of Bible reading and prayer, good counseling, and so on), it is still fundamental because it animates the other instruments. Without a clear grasp of the gospel, I won't be able to take loving critique from others. Without knowing the gospel, I won't be able to meet the Lord in his Word.

Horton's last criticism circles back to my distinction between the gospel's presuppositions and the gospel itself. He says that while I explicitly make this distinction — which he heartily affirms — he wonders if elsewhere I don't violate my own principle. I often say that the gospel "shows us" we are wicked and lost. Horton thinks, rather, that it is the law, not the gospel itself, that shows us our sin. He asks me to clarify this.

I believe the law of God convicts nonbelievers (the "first use") and guides Christians (the "third use"), and it is important to avoid presuming that the gospel does all this on its own. The gospel does not contain the Ten Commandments. Nor could we possibly show the world (and the church) its sin and need of salvation without the Decalogue. Also, it is obvious that the term *gospel* means "good news," not "bad news and good news." So shouldn't we keep things clean and neat and say it is the gospel alone that tells us we are pardoned, saved, and accepted, while it is the law alone that shows us we are sinners? Shouldn't we say, therefore, that every evangelistic presentation is actually a law-and-gospel presentation?

Maybe we should. But if we do, we need to be generous and grant that in both the Bible and real-life ministry, it is natural to say to people, "Here's the gospel to believe" — and to include in that presentation a description of sin. When Paul summarizes in 1 Corinthians 15 what he calls his "gospel" (vv. 1–2), he includes the statement that Christ "died for our sins" (v. 3). Obviously, the good news of salvation makes no sense without some description of what we are being saved from. So Paul includes that in the communication of what he calls "the gospel," and it plays itself out in his actual speeches in the book of Acts. I don't think, therefore, we should overcorrect people who speak (perhaps a bit imprecisely) the way Paul does.

Yet I hear Horton's criticism as an exhortation (e.g., "Keller could offer helpful counsel by clarifying ..." [p. 89]) for me to clearly promote the use of the law of God in preaching as such, to be kept in the closest, most intimate proximity to the gospel, both in the evangelism of nonbelievers and the edification of the saints. If we use the law with power to show people their need for grace, then when we bring in the gospel, it will fall on their ears like the greatest music. I agree with his proposal.

Some might object to this, saying, "Non-Christians in the secular West don't believe in the Bible or the law of God. They are relativists. The 'first use of the law' doesn't work on them." That is only partly true. The truth is that those who don't believe in God's revelation still have a conscience that is still sensitive in some ways to the dictates of the law (Rom 2:15).

Here is just one example. John Calvin has a powerful exposition of the meaning of the second part of the great commandment "love thy neighbor" in light of the teaching of the *imago Dei*:

> The Lord commands all men without exception "to do good" [Heb 13:16]. Yet the great part of them are most unworthy if they be judged by their own merit. But here Scripture helps in the best way when it teaches that we are not to consider that men merit of themselves but to look upon the image of God in all men, to which we owe all honor and love ... Say, "He is contemptible and worthless"; but the Lord shows him to be one to whom he has deigned to give the beauty of his image ... Say that he does not deserve even your least effort for his sake; but the image of God, which recommends him to you, is worthy of your giving yourself and all your possessions ... You will say, "He has deserved something far different of me."

Yet what has the Lord deserved?... Assuredly there is but one way in which to achieve what is not merely difficult but utterly against human nature: to love those who hate us, to repay their evil deeds with benefits, to return blessings for reproaches [Matt 5:44]. It is that we remember not to consider men's evil intention but to look upon the image of God in them, which cancels and effaces their transgressions, and with its beauty and dignity allures us to love and embrace them.[1]

This is a remarkable exhortation. We look at our neighbor, someone who in himself genuinely does not deserve our help or our love, and yet we must give him "what the Lord deserves" because every human being, even the weakest, the most unlovely, or the most twisted, has the mark of God's image. Now most people in the West want to think they believe in human rights and the dignity of all human beings, but they will tune in to this exposition of the law, astonished by its power and beauty. Indeed, they will probably object to it—and not by saying, "Oh, that's just your interpretation! I think it's fine to mistreat people." They won't take the relativist route. No, they will complain that it's *too high a standard*, impossible to attain, even though in their hearts they will admire it and the theology behind it. They will be drawn to it even as they feel it's beyond them. That's called conviction of sin through "the first use of the law." It can be done. It should be done.

Part 2

GOSPEL RENEWAL

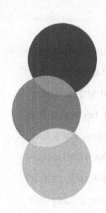

Chapter 4

THE NEED FOR GOSPEL RENEWAL

Gospel renewal is a life-changing recovery of the gospel. *Personal* gospel renewal means the gospel doctrines of sin and grace are actually experienced, not just known intellectually. This personal renewal includes an awareness and conviction of one's own sin and alienation from God and comes from seeing in ourselves deeper layers of self-justification, unbelief, and self-righteousness than we have ever seen before. There is a new, commensurate grasp of the wonder of forgiveness and grace as we shed these attitudes and practices and rest in Christ alone for salvation. Perhaps we have previously said that we were "resting in Christ's work, not our own work" for salvation, but when we experience gospel renewal, we have a new clarity about what this means in our mind and a new experience of actually doing it with our heart.

Corporate gospel renewal—what has sometimes been called "revival"—is a season in which a whole body of believers experience personal gospel renewal together.[1] Over time, all churches, no matter how sound their theology, tend to lose sight of the uniqueness of the gospel and fall into practices that conform more to other religions or to irreligion. Their doctrinal instruction loses sight of how each doctrine plays a role in the gospel message, and their moral instruction is not grounded in and motivated by the finished work and grace of Christ. The leaders of the church must always be bringing the gospel to bear on people's minds and hearts so that they see it as not just a set of beliefs but as a power that changes us profoundly and continually. Without this kind of application of the gospel, mere teaching, preaching, baptizing, and catechizing are not sufficient.

Richard Lovelace was a student of the history of revivals. He sought to discover what, for all their apparent differences, they had in common. He concluded that while Christians know intellectually that their justification (acceptance by God) is the basis for their sanctification (their actual moral behavior), in their actual "day-to-day existence ... they rely on their sanctification for their justification ... drawing their assurance of acceptance with God from their sincerity, their past experience of conversion, their recent religious performance or the relative infrequency of their conscious, willful disobedience."[2]

In other words, revivals and renewals are necessary because the default mode of the human heart is works-righteousness — we do not ordinarily live as if the gospel is true. Christians often believe in their heads that "Jesus accepts me; therefore I will live a good life," but their hearts and actions are functioning practically on the principle "I live a good life; therefore Jesus accepts me." The results of this inversion are smug self-satisfaction (if we feel we are living up to standards) or insecurity, anxiety, and self-hatred (if we feel we are failing to live up). In either case, the results are defensiveness, a critical spirit, racial or cultural ethnocentricity to bolster a sense of righteousness, an allergy to change, and other forms of spiritual deadness, both individual and corporate. In sharp contrast, the gospel of sheer grace offered to hopeless sinners will humble and comfort all at once. The results are joy, a willingness to admit faults, graciousness with all, and a lack of self-absorption.[3]

Because we don't really believe the gospel deep down — because we are living as if we save ourselves — our hearts find ways of either rejecting or reengineering the doctrine (as in liberal theology) or of mentally subscribing to the doctrine while functionally trusting and resting in our own moral and doctrinal goodness (as in "dead orthodoxy"). As a result, individuals and churches experience a slow spiritual deadening over the years, unless some sort of renewal/revival dynamic arrests it.

Revival can be widespread, affecting a whole region or country, or more narrow in scope, influencing just one congregation or even just a part of one. It can be fairly gentle and quiet or rather sensational. But all revivals are seasons in which the ordinary operations of the Holy Spirit are intensified manifold. In revival, the ordinary means of grace produce a great wave of newly awakened inquirers, soundly converted sinners, and spiritually renewed believers. The church growth that inevitably results cannot be accounted for by demographical-sociological shifts or efficient outreach programs.

So revival is not a historical curiosity; it is a consistent pattern of how the Holy Spirit works in a community to arrest and counteract the default mode of the human heart. It is surely relevant to ministry in twenty-first-century global cultures, as it is relevant in every culture.

Critiquing Revivals

We cannot sufficiently cover a full history of revivals here. We know that revivals have often had powerful, society-changing effects.[4] The most famous revival in American history, the Great Awakening of the early and mid-eighteenth century, had a major impact on the culture and history of both Britain and the United States. And of course there have been other well-known revivals in many other parts of the world.[5] Throughout history, revivals have also drawn sharp criticism and suspicion. When William B. Sprague, a Presbyterian minister in Albany, New York, published his lectures on revival in 1832, he devoted his longest lecture to a "Defence of Revivals," fielding several objections and addressing many of the most common criticisms of revival. He addressed concerns that revivals were unbiblical and "modern," that they led to emotional excesses and fanaticism, that they split families, and that they undermined established churches.[6]

This last charge—that revivals undermine the role and importance of the church—is the most persistent today. I want to examine this charge by looking back at the conditions that led to revivalism in the first place. Before the eighteenth century, a person became a Christian through a process that was corporate, gradual, formal, and completely church-centric. First came the presentation of an infant for baptism by the whole family. After that came a long period of catechetical instruction in the church's historical creeds and traditions. Finally, it was expected that the child would be admitted to the Lord's Supper as a full communicant. Weddings and funerals in the church were also significant milestones, all observed with one's family in the presence of the congregation and through forms and traditions that tied all participants in the present to the lives of believers in the past. One's faith was first inherited and then personally confirmed by the individual through a highly communal process that entailed the support and approval of his or her family, church, and religious authorities.

However, the Industrial Revolution brought profound social changes. Many people were displaced to the big cities to work in factories, which took them away from their parish churches and small towns where everyone knew everyone else and where norms of behavior and participation in institutions could be enforced through social pressure. Second, market capitalism gave individuals (who could now act more autonomously) more goods and services to choose from.

The revivalist ministries of the Wesleys in England and of George Whitefield in America were responses to these cultural realities. They took preaching directly to the masses in outdoor meetings that called people to conversion, not waiting for them to be processed by their local parish churches in the traditional way, because (revivalists felt) this was less and less likely to happen. Revivalists emphasized the decisions of individuals rather than the incorporation of families into a community and called on a dramatic turning experience, rather than a process of liturgy and catechism, for spiritual formation.[7]

Now we see why Sprague in the 1830s had to respond to the charges that revivalists were undermining the authority of the ordained ministry and the local church. Detractors of revivals said that, in the long run, stressing conversion and revival undermines churches' ability to instruct and discipline their members. Participation in church comes to be viewed as optional, since salvation comes directly through personal faith and experience—it is not mediated through the church. Emotional experience is placed above doctrinal soundness and holiness of life. Christianity becomes a way to meet felt needs instead of a means of re-forming a person into the image of Christ. The individual is privileged at the expense of the community, so every Christian becomes his or her own spiritual authority, and there is no true accountability.[8]

They were partly right, of course. These criticisms of revivalism hit home in the eighteenth century (and are equally valid today). In fact, Sprague's second-longest lecture was on "Evils to Be Avoided in Connection to Revivals," and here he leveled his own criticisms of the excesses of revivalism, excesses that eventually came to full flower in Charles Finney's ministry.[9] Sprague was part of an influential stream of nineteenth-century Reformed theology that was able to find a middle ground in the debate. Archibald Alexander, the founding faculty member of Princeton Seminary, remained a strong promoter of revivals, despite his recognition of all their possible negative effects. He believed those effects were not inherent to revival and could be avoided or minimized.

Alexander and his successors at Princeton continued to support the basic insights of revival while insisting on the critical importance of both evangelism and spiritual formation. As believers in infant baptism, they understood that baptized children were part of the church and recipients of God's grace in the life of the family through the sacrament. But they continued to exhort children to put their faith in Christ and counseled them about what conversion looked like.[10] When it came time to admit children to the Lord's Supper, they looked for a "credible profession of faith" rather than simply admitting any child who completed church instruction. While continuing to affirm the importance of the church in the process of spiritual formation, they emphasized the ongoing need to preach and teach the gospel message—even to their own children and congregations.

Revivalism Today

The same debate continues today, as the perils of unbalanced revivalism are still apparent in the church. Extreme revivalism is certainly too individualistic. Our truth-allergic, experience-addicted populace wants transformation but doesn't want the loss of freedom and control associated with submitting to authority within a committed community. Many "converts" seem to make decisions for Christ but soon lose their enthusiasm because they are offered quick programs for follow-up and small group fellowship rather than a lifelong, embodied experience of community. Many churches do not even have a process for becoming a member. As a result, converts' lives are often not visibly different from those in the culture around them. The older, more communal processes of traditional churches are better at bringing about a more thorough transformation of life.

However, many of today's critics do more than lament these effects; they deny the basic premises of revival. They reject the idea that we should call people to conversion if they are in the church. Many aim to recapture something similar to the traditional church life of pre-eighteenth-century Europe, where no one could "become a Christian" except through incorporation into a local congregation. And once baptized and incorporated, this person was a Christian by definition, regardless of personal experience.

I believe this is a mistake for two fundamental reasons. To use biblical terms, this position does not know the times and seasons, and it does not sufficiently account for the heart. Or, to put it more positively, the basic insights and practices of gospel renewal ministry are right for two reasons: they fit our times, and they center on the heart in a biblical way.

Gospel renewal fits our times. What do I mean when I say that revival "fits our times"? The traditional, highly church-centered approach worked well when there was one dominant church and religious tradition in a culture and when the private and public sectors put far fuller weight behind the church. The institutions of society and the shared symbols and practices of common life expressed, confirmed, and reinforced religious beliefs. In such an environment, the culture's God seemed inevitable and the worldview of our society's religion seemed plausible to everyone. The traditional model also depended on not having many kinds of churches to choose from. Alternative denominations or religions were absent or were heavily stigmatized. Citizens could choose to be active in their society's inherited faith (and the local parish) or to just be fairly inactive, but those were the only two realistic options. The social realities were such that virtually no one *chose* their own faith, let alone their own congregation.

This church-centric model broke down as people became increasingly mobile and society slowly but surely became more pluralistic. North America was the first place where churches had to *appeal* for members and converts. Americans only came to church if they chose to do so.[11] Now wind the clock forward a couple of centuries to today's pluralistic societies, where the important institutions of our public life do not all point to a unified set of beliefs about life and reality. No one really inherits their belief systems as they once did. People actively choose among competing sets of beliefs and worldviews and must be persuaded through personal appeals to do so.[12] I believe this state of affairs demands the revivalist emphasis on persuasion, conversion, and individual self-examination.

Gospel renewal focuses on the heart. I believe this second reason for retaining the basic insights and practices of revival is the more important one. Revivalism's core insight—that salvation is a matter of the heart—has ample grounding in the Bible. In Romans 10:9, Paul writes, "If you declare with your mouth, 'Jesus is Lord,' and believe in your heart that God raised him from the dead, you will be saved." Virtually all commentaries observe that this means it is not enough to agree with Christian truth intellectually ("declare with your mouth"). There must also be personal trust, a heart conviction.

When the Bible speaks of the heart, it means more than just our emotions. It is true that we feel our emotions in our hearts (Lev 19:17; Pss 4:7; 13:2), but we also think and reason in our hearts (Prov 23:7; Mark 2:8) and even act from our hearts (Eccl 10:2). Our heart is the center of our personality, the seat of our fundamental commitments, the control center of the whole person. What is in the heart determines what we think, do, and feel—since mind, will, and emotions are all rooted there. Paul states in Romans 10:9–10 that it is not enough to grasp and assent rationally to Christian truth, though that is absolutely necessary. Saving faith is never less than intellectual assent, but it is always more than that. It combines rational knowledge with the conviction and trust of the heart.

For an example of revival preaching in the Old Testament, consider Jeremiah's call to the Israelites and his demand to "circumcise your hearts" (Jer 4:4; cf. 9:26; Acts 7:51). Jeremiah's listeners had the outward sign of the covenant, yet Jeremiah informed them they did not have the inward reality of a new heart (Jer 31:33). The rite of circumcision was the sign of belonging to the covenant community. It functioned much like baptism in the Christian church (Col 2:11– 12). Anyone who was circumcised had been visibly incorporated into the community of God's people. And yet, according to Jeremiah, there was more required of them than just the outward signs. Salvation required the removal of a stony heart (Ezek 11:19). The heart had to be cleansed (Ps 51:10) and made steadfast (Ps 112:7).

The New Testament continues to make this distinction between the outward and the inward. In Romans, Paul makes the case that many who were members of God's covenant people "outwardly" were not so "inwardly," because "circumcision is ... of the heart, by the Spirit" (Rom 2:28–29). In his letter to the Philippians, Paul declares that in Christ, Christians become the "[true] circumcision, we who serve God by his Spirit" (Phil 3:3). Here he ties Christian conversion to the "heart circumcision" of the Old Testament.[13] In this chapter, Paul describes his reliance on law keeping and moral attainments ("put no confidence in the flesh"—v. 3) and how he once lacked this inward spiritual reality. The renewal and heart change in Paul's life came only when he transferred his trust from law keeping to Christ's imputed righteousness for his confidence before God (vv. 4b, 7–9). When Jesus called a religious leader to be "born again" by the Holy Spirit (John 3:7), he was making essentially the same exhortation that Jeremiah had made in calling the people to circumcise their hearts.

Another warrant for emphasizing the heart is the biblical teaching on the relationship between repentance and faith. The summary of Jesus' gospel given in Mark 1:15 highlights this relationship: "The kingdom of God has come near. Repent and believe the good news!" In Luke 24:47, Jesus states that "repentance for the forgiveness of sins will be preached in [my] name to all nations, beginning at Jerusalem." And when people ask Peter how to be saved, he tells them to repent (Acts 2:38; see 3:19; 5:31). Repeatedly throughout the New Testament, we see that saving faith and repentance are inseparable and that true repentance includes grief and sorrow over our sin (2 Cor 7:10). Second Corinthians 7:11 tells us that repentance includes zeal, indignation, and longing, using a variety of terms to show that repentance is a deep experience that profoundly affects the mind, will, and emotions. Repentance changes the heart. It will never be enough to ask if a person has learned the faith, has been baptized, or has joined the church. If he or she has not repented, it is all to no avail.

Gospel renewal does not simply seek to convert nominal church members; it also insists that *all* Christians — even committed ones — need the Spirit to bring the gospel home to their hearts for deepened experiences of Christ's love and power. In Paul's great prayer for the Ephesians in chapter 3, he prays for his readers that Christ will dwell in their hearts and they may be filled with all the fullness of God. This is noteworthy, since *he is writing to Christians*, not nonbelievers. By definition, all Christians already have Christ dwelling in them (1 Cor 6:19; Col 1:27) and have the fullness of God (Col 2:9–10) by virtue of their union with Christ through faith. What does Paul mean, then, by his prayer? He must be saying that he hopes the Ephesians will *experience* what they already believe in and possess — the presence and love of Christ (Eph 3:16–19). But how does this experience happen? It comes through the work of the Spirit, strengthening our "inner being" and our "hearts" so that as believers we can know Christ's love (see v. 16). It happens, in other words, through gospel renewal.

This fits perfectly with what Jesus declares about the work of the Holy Spirit in John's gospel: "[The Holy Spirit] will glorify me because it is from me that he will receive what he will make known to you" (John 16:14). The phrase "make known" indicates a momentous announcement, a declaration that grabs attention. The Holy Spirit's job is to unfold the meaning of Jesus' person and work in such a way that its infinite importance and beauty are brought home to the mind and heart. This is why in the letter to the Ephesians Paul hopes that Christians, who already know rationally that Christ loves them, will have "the eyes of [their] heart ... enlightened" (1:18) so they will "have power ... to grasp how wide and long and high and deep is the love of Christ" (3:18). Paul's prayers in Ephesians show that Christians can expect the Holy Spirit to continually renew their boldness, love, joy, and power as they go beyond merely believing in the things that Jesus has done to experiencing them by the work of the Spirit.

● ● ●

Unbalanced revivalism indeed undermines the work of the established church. But balanced revivalism—a commitment to corporate and individual gospel renewal through the ordinary means of grace—*is* the work of the church. This is because it is possible (even common) for a person to be baptized, to be an active member of the church, to subscribe to all biblical doctrines, and to live according to biblical ethics, but nonetheless to be wholly unconverted. Revivalist ministry emphasizes conversion and spiritual renewal, not only for those outside the church, but also for those *inside* the church. Some need to be converted from clear unbelief; others need to see, to their surprise, that they've never been converted; still others need to sense their spiritual stagnation.

In commenting on "the truth of the gospel" (Gal 2:5), Martin Luther says the gospel is for us "the principal article of all Christian doctrine ... Most necessary it is, therefore, that we should know this article well, teach it unto others, and beat it into their heads continually."[14] If it were natural or even possible for our hearts to operate consistently from the truth and in the life-giving power of the gospel, we wouldn't need to have it beat into our heads continually. We wouldn't need a persistent, balanced, revivalist ministry of gospel renewal. But of course it isn't possible; and so we do.

DISCUSSION QUESTIONS

1. Have you ever experienced spiritual renewal in a corporate setting as described in this chapter? If so, how would you describe it? How did it differ from a more personal experience of renewal?

2. What training currently takes place in your church for teaching children and new believers, and what three things could you do differently after reading this chapter?

3. What does it mean to say that "the basic insights and practices of gospel renewal ministry are right for two reasons: they fit our times, and they center on the heart in a biblical way." How does gospel renewal ministry fit our times, and how is it uniquely focused on the heart?

4. How can you bring more of a gospel renewal focus to your existing ministry?

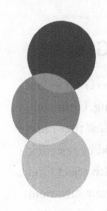

Chapter 5

THE ESSENCE OF GOSPEL RENEWAL

Revival is necessary because religion ("I obey; therefore I am accepted") is so different from the gospel ("I am accepted by God through Christ; therefore I obey") but is such an effective counterfeit. Though these systems of motivation and purpose have utterly different lineages, on the surface they may look like twins. Two people basing their lives on these two systems may sit right beside each other in church. Both strive to obey the law of God, to pray, to give generously, and to be good family members. Yet they do so out of radically different motives, in radically different spirits, and resulting in radically different kinds of inner personal character. One of them (the "religious" one) may even be lost altogether. Even the one operating out of the gospel will naturally drift into religion unless constantly challenged and renewed.

If these insights from the last chapter addressed the *why* of gospel renewal, the question for this chapter is the *what* of gospel renewal. What does the gospel do that actually changes people in a congregation? How can the distinct and unique theological truths of the gospel be formulated in ways that produce new, Spirit-led, Christ-centered motivation in people, whether their starting point is religion or irreligion? First we will look further at the distinction between religion, irreligion, and the gospel. Then we will see how these insights are applied to the heart.

Three Ways of Responding to God

Christians typically identify two ways to respond to God: follow him and do his will, or reject him and do your own thing. Ultimately this is true, but there are actually *two ways to reject God* that must be distinguished from one another. You can reject God by rejecting his law and living any way you see fit. And you can also reject God by embracing and obeying God's law so as to earn your salvation. The problem is that people in this last group—who reject the gospel in favor of moralism—*look* as if they are trying to do God's will. Consequently, there are not just two ways to respond to God but three: irreligion, religion, and the gospel.

Irreligion is avoiding God as Lord and Savior by ignoring him altogether. "Religion," or moralism, is avoiding God as Lord and Savior by developing a moral righteousness and then presenting it to God in an effort to show that he "owes" you.[1] The gospel, however, has nothing to do with our developing a righteousness we give God so he owes us; it is God's developing and giving us righteousness through Jesus Christ (1 Cor 1:30; 2 Cor 5:21). The gospel differs from both religion and irreligion, from both moralism and relativism.

This theme runs the length of the Bible. When God saves the Israelites from slavery in Egypt, he first leads them out and *then* gives them the law to obey. Law obedience is the result of their deliverance and election, not the cause of it (Exod 19:4–5; Deut 7:6–9). As God makes a covenant with the Israelites, he warns them that it is still possible for them to be uncircumcised in heart (Lev 26:41; Deut 10:16; 30:6; Jer 4:4)—even as they are completely compliant and obedient to all the laws, observances, and rituals of worship. As we saw in the previous chapter, it took the New Testament to lay out what it meant to be the true circumcision (Phil 3:3). Paul tells us that the circumcised in heart do not rely on their law keeping for confidence before God. Paul explains the three ways to live according to the Old Testament: (1) literally uncircumcised (pagans and nonbelievers who do not submit to God's laws); (2) circumcised only in the flesh (submitted to God's law but resting and relying on it); and (3) circumcised in heart (submitted to God's law in response to the saving grace of God).

In the New Testament, these three ways appear most prominently in Romans 1–4. Beginning in Romans 1:18–32, Paul shows how the pagan, immoral Gentiles are lost and alienated from God. In Romans 2:1–3:20, Paul counterintuitively states that the moral, Bible-believing Jews are lost and alienated from God as well. "What shall we conclude then? Do we have any advantage? Not at all! For we have already made the charge that Jews and Gentiles alike are all under the power of sin. As it is written: 'There is no one righteous, not even one; there is no one ... who seeks God'" (Rom 3:9–11). The last part of this statement is particularly shocking, since Paul concludes that thousands of men and women who were diligently obeying and believing the Bible were *not seeking* God, even in all their religion. The reason is that if you seek to be right with God through your morality and religion, you are not seeking God for your salvation; you are using God as a means to achieve your own salvation. Paul proceeds in the rest of Romans to explain the gospel as seeking God in Christ for salvation through grace alone and through faith alone.

Throughout the Gospels, these three ways — religion, irreligion, and the gospel — are repeatedly depicted in Jesus' encounters. Whether a Pharisee or a tax collector (Luke 18), a Pharisee or a fallen woman (Luke 7), or a respectable crowd and a man possessed by a demon (Mark 5), in every instance the less moral, less religious person connects more readily to Jesus. Even in John 3 and 4, where a similar contrast occurs between a Pharisee and an immoral Samaritan woman, the woman receives the gospel with joy, while Nicodemus the Pharisee evidently has to go home and think about it. Here we have the New Testament version of what we saw in earlier pages of the Bible—that God chooses the foolish things to shame the wise, the weak things to shame the strong, to show that his salvation is by grace (see 1 Cor 1:26–31).

It is so much easier to move from the gospel to religion than the other way round. One of Martin Luther's fundamental insights is that religion is the default mode of the human heart. Even irreligious people earn their acceptability and sense of worth by living up to their set of values.[2] And the effects of "works-religion" persist so stubbornly in the heart that Christians who believe the gospel at one level will continually revert to religion, operating at deeper levels as if they are saved by their works. Richard F. Lovelace develops this train of thought:

> Only a fraction of the present body of professing Christians are solidly appropriating the justifying work of Christ in their lives. Many … have a theoretical commitment to this doctrine, but in their day-to-day existence they rely on their sanctification for justification … drawing their assurance of acceptance with God from their sincerity, their past experience of conversion, their recent religious performance or the relative infrequency of their conscious, willful disobedience. Few know enough to start each day with a thoroughgoing stand upon Luther's platform: you are accepted, looking outward in faith and claiming the wholly alien righteousness of Christ as the only ground for acceptance, relaxing in that quality of trust which will produce increasing sanctification as faith is active in love and gratitude …
>
> Much that we have interpreted as a defect of sanctification in church people is really an outgrowth of their loss of bearing with respect to justification. Christians who are no longer sure that God loves and accepts them in Jesus, apart from their present spiritual achievements, are subconsciously

radically insecure persons … Their insecurity shows itself in pride, a fierce defensive assertion of their own righteousness and defensive criticism of others. They come naturally to hate other cultural styles and other races in order to bolster their own security and discharge their suppressed anger.[3]

A QUICK COMPARISON OF RELIGION AND THE GOSPEL[4]

RELIGION	GOSPEL
"I obey; therefore I'm accepted."	"I'm accepted; therefore I obey."
Motivation is based on fear and insecurity.	Motivation is based on grateful joy.
I obey God in order to get *things* from God.	I obey God to get *God* — to delight and resemble him.
When circumstances in my life go wrong, I am angry at God or myself, since I believe, like Job's friends, that anyone who is good deserves a comfortable life.	When circumstances in my life go wrong, I struggle, but I know that all my punishment fell on Jesus and that, while he may allow this for my training, he will exercise his fatherly love within my trial.
When I am criticized, I am furious or devastated because it is essential for me to think of myself as a "good person." Threats to that self-image must be destroyed at all costs.	When I am criticized, I struggle, but it is not essential for me to think of myself as a "good person." My identity is not built on my record or my performance but on God's love for me in Christ. I became a Christian by understanding these truths; therefore, in Christ, I can take criticism.
My prayer life consists largely of petition and only heats up when I am in a time of need. My main purpose in prayer is control of the environment.	My prayer life consists of generous stretches of praise and adoration. My main purpose is fellowship with him.

RELIGION	GOSPEL
My self-view swings between two poles. If and when I am living up to my standards, I feel confident, but then I am prone to be proud and unsympathetic to people who fail. If and when I am not living up to standards, I feel humble but not confident — I feel like a failure.	My self-view is not based on a view of myself as a moral achiever. In Christ I am *simul justus et peccator* — simultaneously sinful and lost, yet accepted in Christ. I am so bad he *had* to die for me, and I am so loved he was *glad* to die for me. This leads me to deeper and deeper humility as well as deeper confidence, without either sniveling or swaggering.
My identity and self-worth are based mainly on how hard I work or how moral I am, so I *must* look down on those I perceive as lazy or immoral. I disdain and feel superior to others.	My identity and self-worth are centered on the One who died for his enemies, who was crucified outside the city for me. I am saved by sheer grace, so I *can't* look down on those who believe or practice something different from me. Only by grace am I what I am. I have no inner need to win arguments.
Since I look to my own pedigree or performance for my spiritual acceptability, my heart manufactures idols. It may be my talents, moral record, personal discipline, social status, etc. I absolutely *have* to have them, so they serve as my main hope, meaning, happiness, security, and significance, whatever I may say I believe about God.	I have many good things in my life — family, work, spiritual disciplines, etc., but none of these good things are *ultimate* things to me. None are things I absolutely *have* to have, so there is a limit to how much anxiety, bitterness, and despondency they can inflict on me when they are threatened and lost.

Preaching the Third Way for Everyone

If you are communicating the gospel message, you must not only help listeners distinguish between obeying God and disobeying him; you must also make clear the distinction between obeying God as a means of self-salvation and obeying God out of gratitude for an accomplished salvation. You will have to distinguish between general, moralistic religion and gospel Christianity. You will always be placing three ways to live before your listeners.

The most important way to gain a hearing from postmodern people, confront nominal Christians, wake up "sleepy" Christians, and even delight committed Christians — *all at the same time* — is to preach the gospel as a third way to approach God, distinct from both irreligion and religion. Why? First, many professed Christians are only nominal believers; they are pure "elder brothers" (see Luke 15:11 – 32), and often making this distinction can help to convert them. Second, many genuine Christians are elder broth*erish* — angry, mechanical, superior, insecure — and making this distinction may be the only way to reach them. Third, most postmodern people have been raised in or near churches that are heavily "religious." They have observed how religious people tend to bolster their own sense of worth by convincing themselves they are better than other people, which leads them to exclude and condemn others. Most contemporary nonbelievers have rejected these poisonous fruits of religion, but when they did so, they thought they had rejected Christianity. If they hear you calling them to follow Christ, even if you use biblical language such as "receive Christ and you will be adopted into his family" (see John 1:12 – 13), they will automatically believe you are calling them into the "elder brother," moralistic, religious approach to God. Unless you are constantly and clearly showing them that they have misunderstood the gospel and that you are talking about something else besides religion, they won't be listening for the true gospel.

Some claim that to always strike a note of "grace, grace, grace" in our sermons is not helpful. The objection goes like this: "Surely Pharisaism and moralism are not the current problem in our culture. Rather, our problem is license and antinomianism. People lack a sense of right or wrong. It is redundant to talk about grace all the time to postmodern people." I don't believe this is true. First, unless you point to the "good news" of grace, people won't even be able to *bear* the "bad news" of God's judgment. Second, unless you critique moralism, many irreligious people will not grasp the difference between moralism and what you are offering in the gospel. A deep grasp of the gospel is the antidote to license and antinomianism.

In the end, legalism and relativism in churches are not just equally wrong; they are basically the same thing. They are just different strategies of self-salvation built on human effort. No matter whether a local church is loose about doctrine and winks at sin or is marked by scolding and rigidity, it will lack the power it promises. The only way into a ministry that sees people's lives change, that brings joy and power and electricity without authoritarianism, is through preaching the gospel to deconstruct both legalism and relativism.

Moralistic Behavior Change

People typically try to instill honesty in others this way: "If you lie, you'll get in trouble with God and other people," or, "If you lie, you'll be like those terrible people, those habitual liars, and you are better than that!" What motivations are being encouraged? They are being called to change their behavior out of fear of *punishment* ("you'll get in trouble") and out of *pride* ("you'll be like a dirty liar; you wouldn't want to be like one of them"). Both fear of punishment and pride are essentially self-centered. The root motivation is, then, "Be honest because it will pay off for you." This approach puts pressure on the will and stirs up the ego to more selfishness in order to force a person to curb his or her inclinations to do wrong. We can call this "moralistic behavior change" because its basic argument is this: "Will yourself to change your behavior, and you can save yourself."

Christians who are taught to act morally primarily to escape punishment or to win self-respect and salvation are learning to be moral to serve themselves. At the behavioral level, of course, they may be performing actions of great self-sacrifice. They may be sacrificing time, money, and much more to help the poor, to love their family, or to be faithful to God's law. Yet at a deeper level they are behaving this way so God will bless them, so they can think of themselves as virtuous, charitable persons. They are not loving God for himself. They are not obeying him simply because of his greatness and because he has done so much for them in Christ. Rather, they are using God to get the things they want. They want answered prayers, good health, and prosperity, and they want salvation in the afterlife. So they "do good," not for God's sake or for goodness' sake, but for their own sake. Their behavior is being changed by the power of their own self-interest.

Stirring up self-centeredness in order to get someone to do the right thing does not get at the fundamental self-regard and self-absorption that is the main problem of the human heart. Consequently, it does nothing to address the main cause of the behavior you are trying to change (such as lying). Moralistic behavior change simply manipulates and leverages radical selfishness without challenging it. It tries to use that selfishness against itself by appealing to fear and pride. But while this may have some success in *restraining* the heart's self-centeredness, it does absolutely nothing to *change* it. Indeed, it only confirms its power.

Moralistic behavior change *bends* a person into a different pattern through fear of consequences rather than *melting* a person into a new shape. But this does not work. If you try to bend a piece of metal without the softening effect of heat, it is likely to snap back to its former position. This is why we see people who try to change through moralistic behaviorism find themselves repeatedly lapsing into sins they thought themselves incapable of committing. They can't believe they embezzled or lied or committed adultery or felt so much blind hatred that they lashed out. Appalled at themselves, they say, "I wasn't raised that way!" But they were. For moralistic behaviorism—even deep within a religious environment—continues to nurture the "ruthless, sleepless, unsmiling concentration on self that is the mark of Hell."[5] This is the reason people embezzle, lie, and break promises in the first place. It also explains why churches are plagued with gossip and fighting. Underneath what appears to be unselfishness is great self-centeredness, which has been enhanced by moralistic modes of ministry and is marked by liberal doses of sanctimony, judgmentalism, and spite.

To complete our illustration, if you try to bend metal without the softening effect of heat, it may simply break. Many people, after years of being crushed under moralistic behaviorism, abandon their faith altogether, complaining that they are exhausted and "can't keep it up." But the gospel of God's grace doesn't try to bend a heart into a new pattern; it *melts* it and *re-forms* it into a new shape. The gospel can produce a new joy, love, and gratitude—new inclinations of the heart that eat away at deadly self-regard and self-concentration. Without this "gospel heat"—the joy, love, and gratitude that result from an experience of grace—people will simply snap. Putting pressure on their will may temporarily alter their behavior, but their heart's basic self-centeredness and insecurity remain.

Gospel Behavior Change

In light of all this, let's look at how the Bible calls us to change. In 2 Corinthians 8 and 9, Paul writes to believers to encourage them to give an offering to the poor, but he wants them to do so without a direct command from him. He does not begin by pressuring them into it or asserting his authority as an apostle. He doesn't force their wills by saying, "I'm an apostle and this is your duty to me," or, "God will punish you if you don't do this." Nor does he put pressure directly on their emotions by telling them stories about how deeply the poor are suffering and how much more money the Corinthians have than the sufferers. Instead, Paul vividly and unforgettably writes, "You know the grace of our Lord Jesus Christ, that though he was rich, yet for your sake he became poor, so that you through his poverty might become rich" (2 Cor 8:9). When Paul states, "You know the grace," he is reminding his readers of the grace of God by means of a powerful image, one that shifts Jesus' salvation into the realm of wealth and poverty. He moves their hearts through a spiritual recollection of the gospel. Paul, in essence, urges, "Think about his costly grace, until the gospel changes you from the heart into generous people."

We find another example in Ephesians, where Paul is addressing spouses — but particularly, it seems, husbands (Eph 5:25 – 33). Many of these men had no doubt retained attitudes and understandings of marriage from their pagan backgrounds, attitudes in which marriage was primarily a business relationship that entailed marrying as profitably as they could. In his letter, Paul wants not only to encourage husbands to be sexually faithful but also to cherish and honor their wives. Here again (as in 2 Cor 8 and 9), Paul exhorts his readers to change their lives by showing unloving husbands the salvation of Jesus, our ultimate Spouse in the gospel, who showed sacrificial love toward us, his "bride." He did not love us because we were lovely (5:25 – 27), but to make us lovely.

In his letter to Titus, Paul calls his readers to "say 'No' to ungodliness and worldly passions, and to live self-controlled, upright and godly lives" (Titus 2:12).[6] Think for a moment of all the ways you can say no to ungodly behavior. You can say:

No — because I'll look bad.

No — because I'll be excluded from the social circles I want to belong to.

No — because then God will not give me health, wealth, and happiness.

No — because God will send me to hell.

No — because I'll hate myself in the morning and lose my self-respect.

Virtually all of these incentives use self-centered impulses of the heart to force compliance to external rules, but they do very little to *change* the heart itself. The motive behind them is not love for God. It is a way of using God to get beneficial things: self-esteem, prosperity, or social approval.

Paul does not urge his readers to use any of these arguments to attempt to change themselves. In the Titus passage, how does he call Christians to gain self-control? Paul states that it is the "grace of God ... that offers salvation ... [that] teaches us to say 'No' to ungodliness" (Titus 2:11–12). In Titus 3:5, Paul explains what he means by this grace: "[God] saved us, not because of righteous things we had done, but because of his mercy." Paul is saying that if you want true change, you must let the gospel *teach* you. This word we translate *teach* is a Greek word that means to train, discipline, and coach someone over a period of time. In other words, you must let the gospel argue with you. You must let the gospel sink down deeply until it changes your views and the structures of your motivation. You must be trained and discipled by the gospel.

The gospel, if it is truly believed, helps us out of the extreme neediness that is natural to the human heart. We have the *need* to be constantly respected, to be appreciated, and to be highly regarded. We *need* to control our lives—not trusting God or anyone else with them. We *need* to have power over others in order to boost our self-esteem. The image of our glorious God delighting over us with all his being (Isa 62:4; Zeph 3:14; cf. Deut 23:5; 30:9)—if this is a mere concept to us, then our needs will overwhelm us and drive our behavior. Without the power of the Spirit, our hearts don't really believe in God's delight or grace, so they operate in their default mode. But the truths of the gospel, brought home by the Spirit, slowly but surely help us grasp in a new way how safe and secure, how loved and accepted, we are in Christ. Through the gospel, we come to base our identity not on what *we* have achieved but on what has been achieved for us in Christ.

And when the gospel, brought home to our hearts (see Eph 3:16–19), eats away at this sin-born neediness, it destroys the inner engines that drive sinful behavior. We don't have to lie, because our reputation isn't so important to us. We don't have to respond in violent anger against opponents, because no one can touch our true treasure. The gospel destroys both the pride and the fearfulness that fuel moralistic behavior change. The gospel destroys *pride*, because it tells us we are so lost that Jesus had to die for us. And it also destroys *fearfulness*, because it tells us that nothing we can do will exhaust his love for us. When we deeply embrace these truths, our hearts are not merely restrained but changed. Their fundamental orientation is transformed.

We no longer act morally simply because it profits us or makes us feel better about ourselves. Instead, we tell the truth and keep our promises simply out of love for the One who died for us, who kept a promise despite the unfathomable suffering it brought him. The gospel leads us to do the right thing not for our sake but for God's sake, for Christ's sake, out of a desire to know, resemble, please, and love the One who saved us. This kind of motivation can only grow in a heart deeply touched by grace.

The Bible's solution to stinginess, then, is a reorientation to the gospel and the generosity of Christ, who poured out his wealth for us (2 Cor 8:9). We don't have to worry about money, because the cross proves God's care for us and gives us security. Likewise, the Bible's solution to a bad marriage is a reorientation to the radical, spousal love of Christ communicated in the gospel. "You shall not commit adultery" (Exod 20:14) makes sense in the context of his spousal love, especially on the cross, where he was completely faithful to us. Only when we know this sacrificial, spousal love of Christ will we have real fortitude to combat lust. His love is fulfilling, so it keeps us from looking to sexual fulfillment to give us what only Jesus can.

What will truly make us sexually faithful spouses or generous persons or good parents or faithful children is *not* a redoubled effort to follow the example of Christ. Rather, it is deepening our understanding of the salvation of Christ and living out of the changes this understanding makes in our hearts—the seat of our minds, wills, and emotions. Faith in the gospel restructures our motivations, our self-understanding, our identity, and our view of the world. It changes our hearts.[7]

Behavioral compliance to rules without heart change will be superficial and fleeting. The purpose of preaching, pastoring, counseling, instructing, and discipling is, therefore, to show people these practical implications of faith in the gospel.

The Importance of Idolatry

One of the most important biblical and practical ways to help people come to see how they fail to believe the gospel is by instructing them on the nature of idolatry.[8] In his *Treatise on Good Works,* an exposition of the Ten Commandments, Martin Luther states that the call to "have no other gods before me" (Exod 20:3) and the call to believe in Jesus alone for our justification (Rom 3–4) are, in essence, the same thing. To say we must have no other gods but God and to say we must not try to achieve our salvation without Christ are one and the same: "Now this is the work of the First Commandment, which commands: 'Thou shalt have no other gods,' which means: 'Since I alone am God, thou shalt place all thy confidence, trust and faith on Me alone, and on no one else.'"[9]

Luther's teaching is this: Anything we look to *more* than we look to Christ for our sense of acceptability, joy, significance, hope, and security is by definition our god—something we adore, serve, and rely on with our whole life and heart. In general, idols can be *good* things (family, achievement, work and career, romance, talent, etc.—even gospel ministry) that we turn into *ultimate* things to give us the significance and joy we need. Then they drive us into the ground because we must have them. A sure sign of the presence of idolatry is inordinate anxiety, anger, or discouragement when our idols are thwarted. So if we lose a good thing, it makes us sad, but if we lose an idol, it devastates us.

Luther also concludes from his study of the commandments that we never break one of the other commandments unless we are also breaking the first.[10] We do not lie, commit adultery, or steal unless we first make something else more fundamental to our hope and joy and identity than God. When we lie, for example, our reputation (or money or whatever) is at that moment more foundational to our sense of self and happiness than the love of Christ. If we cheat on our income tax form, then money and possessions—and the status or comfort from having more of them—have become more important to our heart's sense of significance and security than our identity in Christ. Idolatry, then, is also the root of our other sins and problems.[11]

So if the root of every sin is idolatry, and idolatry is a failure to look to Jesus for our salvation and justification, then the root of every sin is a failure to believe the gospel message that Jesus, and *Jesus alone*, is our justification, righteousness, and redemption.

What, then, is the essence of behavior change? What will help us lead godly lives? The solution is not simply to force or scare ourselves into doing the right thing, but to apply the gospel to our hearts' idols, which are always an alternate form of self-salvation apart from Jesus. Our failures in *actual* righteousness, then, generally come from a failure to rejoice in our *legal* righteousness in Christ. Our failures in sanctification (living Christlike, godly lives) come mainly from a lack of orientation to our justification. We will never change unless we come to grips with the particular, characteristic ways our hearts resist the gospel and continue their self-salvation projects through idolatry.

Those who preach and counsel for gospel renewal should constantly speak about underlying idols, which show us our hearts' particular, characteristic ways of failing to believe the gospel. To do so will prevent people from trying to solve all problems and make all changes through moralistic behaviorism, which leads to insecurity, suppressed anger and guilt, and spiritual deadness.[12] Instead it keeps the focus on the gospel and the work of Christ. In the next chapter, we'll look at how churches can cooperate with the Holy Spirit to bring about gospel renewal.

DISCUSSION QUESTIONS

1. How would you articulate the three ways of responding to God? What are the differences and similarities between the two ways of rejecting God? How do both of these contrast with a response to the gospel?

2. Where do you find yourself in the chart titled "A Quick Comparison of Religion and the Gospel"? Go back and honestly take stock: Do the majority of your descriptors fall to the left

column or to the right? In what situations do you find yourself turning to religion instead of the gospel? How have your patterns changed over the last five years, and why?

3. Keller writes, "The only way into a ministry that sees people's lives change, that brings joy and power and electricity without authoritarianism, is through preaching the gospel to deconstruct both legalism and relativism." Why is it necessary to confront and deconstruct both of these errors? Which is more prevalent in your context? Which are you more likely to confront, and what can you do to restore balance to your ministry?

4. The apostle Paul uses pictures of the gospel rather than pressure to lead people to change. This chapter gives three examples (generosity, husbands honoring wives, and self-control). Choose another area of life change and take notes on how you would bring the gospel to bear on the motivation of someone in your congregation. If you are in a group setting, practice this with someone else.

Chapter 6

THE WORK OF GOSPEL RENEWAL

We have talked about the *need* for gospel renewal and the *essence* of the gospel in revival and renewal, and now we will look at the *work* of gospel renewal—the practical ways and means by which the Holy Spirit brings lasting change to the lives of individuals and to congregations.

We will also focus in more detail on one of these means—the work of preaching—and examine several signs that give evidence of gospel renewal.

The Means of Gospel Renewal

While the ultimate source of a revival is the Holy Spirit, the Spirit ordinarily uses several "instrumental," or penultimate, means to produce revival.

Extraordinary Prayer

To kindle every revival, the Holy Spirit initially uses what Jonathan Edwards called "extraordinary prayer"—united, persistent, and kingdom centered. Sometimes it begins with a single person or a small group of people praying for God's glory in the community. What is important is not the number of people praying but the nature of the praying. C. John Miller makes a helpful and perceptive distinction between "maintenance" and "frontline" prayer meetings.[1] Maintenance prayer meetings are short, mechanical, and focused on physical needs inside the church. In contrast, the three basic traits of frontline prayer are these:

1. A request for grace to confess sins and to humble ourselves
2. A compassion and zeal for the flourishing of the church and the reaching of the lost
3. A yearning to know God, to see his face, to glimpse his glory

These distinctions are unavoidably powerful. If you pay attention at a prayer meeting, you can tell quite clearly whether these traits are present. In the biblical prayers for revival in Exodus 33; Nehemiah 1; and Acts 4, the three elements of frontline prayer are easy to see. Notice in Acts 4, for example, that after the disciples were threatened by the religious authorities, they asked not for protection for themselves and their families but only for boldness to keep preaching! Some kind of extraordinary prayer beyond the normal services and patterns of prayer is always involved.

Gospel Rediscovery

Along with extraordinary, persistent prayer, the most necessary element of gospel renewal is *a recovery of the gospel itself*, with a particular emphasis on the new birth and on salvation through grace alone. D. Martyn Lloyd-Jones taught that the gospel emphasis on grace could be lost in several ways. A church might simply become heterodox—losing its grip on the orthodox tenets of theology that undergird the gospel, such as the triune nature of God, the deity of Christ, the wrath of God, and so on. It may turn its back on the very belief in justification by faith alone and the need for conversion and so move toward a view that being a Christian is simply a matter of church membership or of living a life based on Christ's example. This cuts the nerve of gospel renewal and revival.[2]

But it is possible to subscribe to every orthodox doctrine and nevertheless fail to communicate the gospel to people's hearts in a way that brings about repentance, joy, and spiritual growth. One way this happens is through dead orthodoxy, in which such pride grows in our doctrinal correctness that sound teaching and right church practice become a kind of works-righteousness. Carefulness in doctrine and life is, of course, critical, but when it is accompanied in a church by self-righteousness, mockery, disdain of everyone else, and a contentious, combative attitude, it shows that, while the doctrine of justification may be believed, a strong spirit of legalism reigns nonetheless. The doctrine has failed to touch hearts.[3]

Lloyd-Jones also speaks of "defective orthodoxy" and "spiritual inertia."[4] Some churches hold to orthodox doctrines but with imbalances and a lack of proper emphasis. Many ministries spend more time defending the faith than propagating it. Or they may give an inordinate amount of energy and attention to matters such as prophecy or spiritual gifts or creation and evolution. A church may become enamored with the mechanics of ministry and church organization. There are innumerable reasons that critical doctrines of grace and justification and conversion, though strongly held, are kept "on the shelf." They are not preached and communicated in such a way that connects to people's lives. People see the doctrines—yet they do not see them. It is possible to get an "A" grade on a doctrinal test and describe accurately the doctrines of our salvation, yet be blind to their true implications and power. In this sense, there are plenty of orthodox churches in which the gospel must be rediscovered and then brought home and applied to people's hearts. When this happens, nominal Christians get converted, lethargic and weak Christians become empowered, and nonbelievers are attracted to the newly beautified Christian congregation.

One of the main vehicles that sparked the first awakening in Northampton, Massachusetts, was Jonathan Edwards's two sermons on Romans 4:5 ("Justification by Faith Alone") in November 1734. And for both John Wesley and George Whitefield, the primary leaders of the British Great Awakening, it was an understanding of salvation by grace *rather* than moral effort that touched off personal renewal and made them agents of revival.

Gospel Application

How do we bring the gospel home to people so they see its power and implications? This can take place in a church in several ways. First, a church recovers the gospel through preaching. Preaching is the single venue of information and teaching to which the greatest number of church people are exposed. Are some parts of the Bible "better" for gospel preaching than others? No, not at all. Any time you preach Christ and his salvation as the meaning of the text rather than simply expounding biblical principles for life, you are preaching toward renewal. Preaching this way is not at all easy, however. Even those who commit to Christ-centered preaching tend toward inspirational sermons about Jesus, with little application. Realizing this is an enormous topic to digest, I point you to Bryan Chapell's *Christ-Centered Preaching*[5] for a place to begin your study. The section titled "Preaching for Gospel Renewal" below also provides more on this subject.

The second way for a pastor or leader to recover the gospel in the church is through the training of lay leaders who minister the gospel to others. It is critical to arrange a regular and fairly intense time of processing these gospel renewal dynamics with the lay leaders of a church. The components of this training include both content and life contact. By "content," I propose studying elementary material such as D. Martyn Lloyd-Jones's chapter "The True Foundation" in

Spiritual Depression or working through my book *The Prodigal God* along with the discussion guide.[6] More advanced materials would include books by Richard Lovelace and Jonathan Edwards.[7]

By "life contact," I mean finding ways in personal meetings and counseling to help your leaders repent of idols and self-righteousness. Once the gospel "penny drops" and begins its ripple effects, you will have plenty of this type of pastoral work to do. Your leaders can then begin leading groups in which they guide people to the truths in the Bible that have helped them and have changed their lives.[8]

A third way for a church to foster gospel renewal dynamics is to inject an experiential element into its small group ministry or even to form several groups dedicated to it. Many small group meetings resemble classes in which the Bible is studied or fellowship meetings in which people talk about their burdens and needs, help each other, and pray for each other. While these functions are extremely important, we can learn from leaders of the revivals of the past, such as George Whitefield and John Wesley, who encouraged people to form groups of four to eight people to share weekly the degree to which God was real in their hearts, their besetting sins, ways God was dealing with them through the Word, and how their prayer lives were faring. *The Experience Meeting* by William Williams is a classic guide to how a Welsh *seiat* or "experience meeting" ran.[9]

A fourth way the gospel becomes applied to people's hearts in a church is through the most basic and informal means possible — what the older writers simply called "conversation." Gospel renewal in the church spreads through renewed individuals talking informally to others. It is in personal conversations that the gospel can be applied most specifically and pointedly. When one Christian shares how the gospel has "come home" to him or her and is bringing about major life changes, listeners can ask concrete questions and receive great encouragement to move forward spiritually themselves. William Sprague writes, "Many a Christian has had occasion ... to reflect that much of his usefulness and much of his happiness was to be referred under God ... to a single conversation with some judicious Christian friend."[10] Sprague states that it is often not so much the actual content of what a Christian says but their gospel-renewed spirit and character that has an impact. Christians must have the infectious marks of spiritual revival—a joyful, affectionate seriousness and "unction," a sense of God's presence.[11] Visible, dramatic life turnarounds and unexpected conversions may cause others to do deep self-examination and create a sense of spiritual longing and expectation in the community. The personal revivals going on in these individuals spread informally to others through conversation and relationship. More and more people begin to examine themselves and seek God.

A fifth way to do gospel application is to make sure that pastors, elders, and other church leaders know how to use the gospel on people's hearts in pastoral counseling—especially people who are coming under a deep conviction of sin and are seeking counsel about how to move forward. Sprague shows how the gospel must be used on seekers, new believers, and stagnant Christians alike.[12] For example, Sprague tells pastoral counselors to "determine ... what is his amount of knowledge and his amount of feeling."[13] He tells counselors to help those who have little doctrinal knowledge but much feeling—or little feeling but a good grasp on doctrine—to bring those two things into balance. Sprague advises to look for forms of self-righteousness and works-righteousness and tells how to help people escape them. He also makes a surprisingly up-to-date list of common doubts and problems that spiritual seekers have and gives advice on how to respond to each one. The gospel must be used to cut away *both* the moralism and the licentiousness that destroy real spiritual life and power.[14]

Gospel Innovation

We can identify another important factor in movements of gospel renewal—creativity and innovation. Sprague rightly points out that revivals occur mainly through the "instituted means of grace"—preaching, pastoring, worship, and prayer. It is extremely important to reaffirm this. The Spirit of God can and does use these ordinary means of grace to bring about dramatic, extraordinary conversions and significant church growth. Nevertheless, when we study the history of revivals, we usually see in the mix some innovative method of communicating the gospel. The Great Awakening of the eighteenth century adopted two ministry forms that had seldom been used: public, outdoor preaching and extensive small group "society" meetings. In the 1857–1859 New York City revival, massive numbers of people were converted and joined the churches of Manhattan. Yet the most vital ministry form turned out to be lay-led, weekday prayer meetings all around the business district of Wall Street. Many historians have pointed out that the Protestant Reformation in Europe was greatly powered by new uses of a major technological innovation—the printing press.

No revival will completely repeat the experiences of the past, and it would be a mistake to identify any specific method too closely with revivals. D. Martyn Lloyd-Jones points to a few sad cases where people who came through the Welsh revival of 1904–1905 became wedded to particular ways of holding meetings and hymn singing as the *only* way that God brings revival. (This kind of nostalgia for beloved methods abounds yet today.) Instead, while the core means of revival are theological (rediscovery of the gospel) and ordinary (preaching, prayer, fellowship, worship), we should always be looking for new modes of gospel proclamation that the Holy Spirit can use in our cultural moment. As C. S. Lewis noted in The Chronicles of Narnia, things never happen the same way twice, so it is best to keep your eyes open.

Preaching for Gospel Renewal

Let's return to our discussion of preaching's role in gospel renewal, for it can hardly be overemphasized. We'll begin by looking at five characteristics that define preaching for gospel renewal.

1. Preach to distinguish between religion and the gospel. We have already laid out much of this imperative in the previous chapter. Effective preaching for gospel renewal will critique both religion and irreligion. It will also address the core problem of idolatry by helping listeners look beneath the level of behavior to their hearts' motivation to see the way the gospel functions (or does not function) in the human heart.

2. Preach both the holiness and the love of God to convey the richness of grace. Preaching should not emphasize only God's judgment, holiness, and righteousness (like moralistic preachers) or emphasize only God's love and mercy (like liberal preachers). Only when people see God as absolutely holy *and* absolutely loving will the cross of Jesus truly electrify and change them. Jesus was so holy that he *had* to die for us; nothing less would satisfy his holy and righteous nature. But he was so loving that he was *glad* to die for us; nothing less would satisfy his desire to have us as his people. This humbles us out of our pride and self-centeredness yet at the same time affirms us out of our discouragement. It leads us to hate sin yet at the same time forbids us to morbidly hate ourselves.

3. Preach not only to make the truth clear but also to make it real. We have seen how Paul seeks greater generosity from people by appealing to them to *know* the grace and generosity of Christ (2 Cor 8). In other words, if Christians are materialistic, it is not merely a failure of will. Their lack of generosity comes because they have not *truly* understood how Jesus became poor for them, how in him we have all true riches and treasures. They may have a superficial intellectual grasp of Jesus' spiritual wealth, but they do not truly, deeply grasp it. Preaching, then, must not simply tell people what to do. It must re-present Christ in such a way that he captures the heart and imagination more than material things. This takes not just intellectual argumentation but the presentation of the *beauty* of Christ.

For Jonathan Edwards, the main spiritual problem for most Christians is that while they have an intellectual grasp of many doctrines, these are not real to their hearts and thus do not influence their behavior.[15] In the case of materialism, the power of money to bring security is more "spiritually real" to people than the security of God's loving and wise providence. Clear preaching, then, is a means to the end of making the truth more real to the hearts of the listeners than it has been before. D. Martyn Lloyd-Jones summarizes it this way:

> The first and primary object of preaching ... is to produce an impression. It is the impression at the time that matters, even more than what you can remember subsequently ... Edwards, in my opinion, has the true notion of preaching. It is not primarily to impart information; and while [the listeners are taking] notes you may be missing something of the impact of the Spirit. As preachers we must not forget this. We are not merely imparters of information. We should tell our people to read certain books themselves and get the information there. The business of preaching is to make such knowledge live.[16]

4. Preach Christ from every text. The main way to avoid moralistic preaching is to be sure that you always preach Jesus as the ultimate point and message of every text. If you don't point listeners to Jesus before the end of the sermon, you will give them the impression that the sermon is basically about *them*—about what they must do. However, we know from texts such as Luke 24:13–49 that Jesus understood every part of the Bible as pointing to him and his saving work. This is not to suggest that the author of every biblical passage intentionally made references to Jesus but that if you put any text into its full, canonical context, it is quite possible to discern the lines that point forward to Christ.

For example, in Judges 19, we have the jarring account of a Levite who is surrounded by violent men in an alien city and who, in order to save his own life, offers his concubine (a second-class wife) to them to gang-rape. There is no way to preach this without talking about the fact that this is a horrible, direct contradiction of all that the Bible demonstrates a husband should be. A husband must protect his wife—and beyond that, he is to sacrifice himself for his wife (Eph 5). And how do we know what a true husband should be? Well, the author of Judges doesn't know it as clearly as we do, but we know what a true husband is when we look at Jesus; Paul writes about this in Ephesians 5. And therefore we must bring the sermon forward to Christ. Only he shows us what husbands should be like, and only when we recognize his saving work can we be free from the fear and pride that makes us bad spouses. This message convicts, but it also gives deep encouragement. We are not trying to desperately earn our salvation by being good spouses; we are applying an accomplished and full salvation to our marriage. We must always turn to Jesus in our sermon because we want to put what the Bible declares in *any one particular place* into context with what the Bible says about it *as a whole*. And this journey always leads us through the gospel to Jesus.

There are, in the end, only two questions to ask as we read the Bible: Is it about me? Or is it about Jesus? In other words, is the Bible basically about what *I* must do or about what *he* has done? Consider the story of David and Goliath. If I read David and Goliath as a story that gives me an example to follow, then the story is really about me. It is an exhortation that *I* must summon up the faith and courage to fight the giants in my life. But if I accept that the Bible is ultimately about the Lord and his salvation, and if I read the David and Goliath text in that light, it throws a multitude of things into sharp relief! The very point of the Old Testament passage is that the Israelites could *not* face the giant themselves. Instead, they needed a champion who would fight in their place—a substitute who would face the deadly peril in their stead. And the substitute that God provided is not a strong person but a weak one—a young boy, too small to wear a suit of armor. Yet God used the deliverer's weakness as the very means to bring about the destruction of the laughing, overconfident Goliath. David triumphs through his weakness and his victory is imputed to his people. And so does Jesus. It is through his suffering, weakness, and death that sin is defeated. This vivid and engaging story shows us what it means to declare that we have died with Christ (Rom 6:1–4) and are raised up and seated with him (Eph 2:5–6). Jesus is the ultimate champion, our *true* champion, who did not merely risk his life for us, but who gave it. And now his victory is our victory, and all he has accomplished is imputed to us.

5. Preach to both Christians and non-Christians at once. When I first came to New York City in the late 1980s, I realized I had not come to a normal part of the United States. Thirty percent of Manhattan residents said they had "no religious preference" compared with (at the time) 6 percent of U.S. residents. Only 5 percent of Manhattanites attended any Protestant church, compared with 25 percent of Americans.[17] I realized that New York City was, religiously and culturally, more like secular, post-Christian Europe. So I looked at the work of Dr. Lloyd-Jones, one of the great preachers who had labored in London in the mid-twentieth century, and I reread his book *Preaching and Preachers*. In addition, I listened to scores (eventually hundreds, I think) of his sermon recordings.

I found particularly fascinating the structure he designed for his preaching. Lloyd-Jones planned his evening sermons to be evangelistic, while the morning sermons were intended to instruct and build up Christians. The evening sermons contained direct appeals to people to come to Christ and believe the gospel but were still richly theological and expository. On the other hand, while the morning sermons assumed a bit more knowledge of Christianity, they always returned to the clear themes of sin, grace, and Christ—the gospel. Lloyd-Jones urged his church members to attend both services. While he saw the evening service as an ideal setting to which to bring a nonbelieving friend, he wanted the professing Christians to attend regularly for their own good. Nor was he concerned when nonbelievers showed up regularly at the morning services. In fact, he wrote, "We must be careful not to be guilty of too rigid a classification of people saying, 'These are Christians, therefore ...' [or] 'Yes, we became Christians as the result of a decision we took at an evangelistic meeting and now, seeing that we are Christians, all we need is teaching and edification.' I contest that very strongly."[18] I learned these lessons from him: Don't just preach to your congregation for spiritual growth, assuming that everyone in attendance is a Christian; and don't just preach the gospel evangelistically, thinking that Christians cannot grow from it. Evangelize as you edify, and edify as you evangelize.

The Signs of Renewal

Revival occurs as a group of people who, on the whole, *think* they already know the gospel discover they do *not* really or fully know it, and by embracing the gospel they cross over into living faith. When this happens in any extensive way, an enormous release of energy occurs. The church stops basing its justification on its sanctification. The nonchurched see this and are attracted by the transformed life of the Christian community as it grows into its calling to be a sign of the kingdom, a beautiful alternative to a human society without Christ.

Often, the first visible sign of renewal is when nominal church members become converted. Nominal Christians begin to realize they had never understood the gospel, experienced the new birth, or entered a living relationship with Christ by grace. Congregations are electrified as longtime church members speak of their conversions, talk about Christ in radiant terms, or express repentance in new ways. These early adopters of renewal stir up other church members into renewal. Soon, "sleepy" Christians also begin to receive a new assurance of and appreciation for grace. They wake up to the reasons they have been living in anxiety, envy, anger, and boredom. They gain a sense of God's reality in the heart as well as higher, immediate assurances of his love. Along with a new and deeper conviction of sin and repentance—concerning not only major behavioral sins but inner attitudes—they have a far more powerful assurance of the nearness and love of God. The deeper their sense of sin debt, the more intense their sense of wonder at Christ's payment of it. As a result, they become simultaneously humbler and bolder.

Of course, the church also begins to see non-Christian outsiders converted as people are attracted to the newly beautified church and its authentic worship, its service in the community, and the surprising absence of condemning, tribal attitudes. Christians become radiant and attractive witnesses—more willing and confident to talk to others about their faith, more winsome and less judgmental when they do so, and more confident in their own church and thus more willing to invite people to visit it. The resulting conversions—sound, lasting, and sometimes dramatic—generate significant, sometimes even astounding, church growth.

Richard Lovelace describes a phenomenon common to churches before and after awakenings and revivals. Ordinarily, various Christian traditions and denominations tend to strongly emphasize one or two ministry functions while being weaker in others. For example, Presbyterians are historically strong in teaching and doctrine, Pentecostals and Anglicans (in their own ways!) in worship, Baptists in evangelism, Anabaptists in community and care for the poor, and so on. During times of gospel renewal, however, these strengths are often combined in churches that are otherwise one-sided. Churches experiencing gospel renewal find that some of the "secondary elements"—areas that typically fell outside of their primary focus—emerge during gospel renewal.[19]

This change is often first felt in the vibrancy of a church's *worship*. When the gospel "comes home"—when both God's holiness and his love become far more magnificent, real, and affecting to the heart—it leads naturally to a new "God reality" in worship. Irrespective of the mode or tradition, renewed churches worship in a way that is no longer one-dimensional—neither merely emotional nor merely formal. A clear, widely felt sense of God's transcendence permeates worship services, which edifies believers while also attracting and helping nonbelievers.

In addition, renewed interest in the gospel always piques interest in an expression of *biblical theology* that is deeply connected to real life. During revival, liberal-leaning churches may grow more biblical, while fundamentalist-leaning churches may grow less sectarian and more focused on the gospel itself rather than on denominational distinctives.

When the gospel comes home—when believers no longer have to maintain their image as competent and righteous—it naturally breaks down barriers that impede relationships and leads to more authentic experiences of *community* with others. Pretense and evasion become unnecessary. The gospel also creates a humility that makes believers empathetic and patient with others. All of this enables relationships within the church to thicken and deepen. During times of renewal, the distinct countercultural nature of the church becomes attractive to outsiders.

Finally, gospel renewal will produce people who are humbled (and thus not disdainful or contemptuous toward those who disagree with them) yet loved (and thus less concerned about others' opinions of them). Therefore every believer becomes a natural evangelist. Times of renewal are always times of remarkable church growth, not through membership transfer and "church shopping," but through conversion. There is also a renewed emphasis on poverty and justice ministries. When Christians realize they did not save themselves but were rescued from spiritual poverty, it naturally changes their attitudes toward people who are in economic and physical poverty. This kind of humble concern is the message of James 1–2 and many other biblical texts. Christians renewed by the gospel render sacrificial service to neighbors, the poor, and the community and city around them.

All of these changes, both within the church and the surrounding community, will eventually have a broad effect on the culture. Gospel-shaped believers who belong to churches that are experiencing gospel renewal often have a deep, vital, and healthy impact on the arts, business, government, media, and academy of any society. The past two decades have produced a far greater acknowledgment that major social justice and social change movements in Britain and the United States—such as the abolition of slavery and the strengthening of child labor laws—had strong roots in the revivals. Because true religion is not merely a private practice that provides internal peace and fulfillment, holiness affects both the private and civic lives of Christians. It transforms behavior and relationships. The active presence of a substantial number of genuine Christians thus changes a community in all its dimensions—economic, social, political, intellectual, and more.

Notice the interdependence of these "secondary elements" flowing naturally from hearts renewed by the gospel. First, many individuals are renewed by the gospel because they are drawn into a church marked by these qualities. Second, the vitality of each factor depends not only on the gospel-renewed heart but also on each of the other factors. They stimulate each other. For example, as

Christians give their lives sacrificially for the poor, their neighbors become more open to evangelism. Deep, rich community could be said to *result* from gospel evangelism, but just as frequently it is a *means* to evangelism, because it makes the gospel credible. Often it is not through listening to preaching but listening to friends that brings us home spiritually. Although these factors are mutually strengthening, the specialists and proponents of each element will almost always pit them against the others. Thus, evangelists may fear that a social justice emphasis will drain energy, attention, and resources from evangelism. Social justice advocates, on the other hand, often resist an emphasis on cultural renewal because they maintain that Christians should be out in the streets identifying with the poor rather than trying to influence the elite worlds of art, media, and business. Community-focused leaders often view rapid church growth and evangelistic programs negatively because they do not like programs—they want everything to happen naturally and "organically." Leaders who grasp how the gospel inspires all of these dimensions must overcome these tensions, and we will discuss these dynamics in greater depth in later chapters.

When the dynamics of gospel renewal are not in place, a church may increase in numbers but not in vitality. It may grow but fail to produce real fruit that has lasting results. It will exhibit symptoms of lifelessness. Most or all of the growth will happen through transfer, not conversion. Because no deep conviction of sin or repentance occurs, few people will attest to dramatically changed lives. Church growth, if it does occur, will make no impact on the local social order because its participants do not carry their Christian faith into their work, their use of monetary resources, or their public lives. However, with these gospel renewal dynamics strong in our hearts and in our churches, our lives and our congregations will be empowered and made beautiful by the Spirit of God.

● ● ●

Of all the elements of a Center Church theological vision, gospel renewal may be the single most difficult one to put into practice because, ultimately, we can only prepare for revival; we can't really bring it about. God must send it. That may discourage those of us who live in a technological society in which we seek to control everything through our competence and will. When we do not see renewal happening, we can get deeply discouraged. But we should not be. Derek Kidner's commentary on Psalm 126 can help us here. The first three verses of Psalm 126 look back to times of great spiritual flourishing, when the Israelites' "mouths were filled with laughter" (v. 2) and when all the nations around them said, "The LORD has done great things for them." But verse 4 tells us that times have changed. The people cry, "Restore our fortunes, LORD." Kidner looks closely at the final parts of the psalm:

> [4]Restore our fortunes, LORD,
>   like streams in the Negev.
> [5]Those who sow with tears
>   will reap with songs of joy.
> [6]Those who go out weeping,
>   carrying seed to sow,
> will return with songs of joy,
>   carrying sheaves with them.

Kidner sees two very different pictures of how revival and renewal can come. The first is in verse 4b; it is "all suddenness, a sheer gift from heaven." Few places are more arid than the Negev, where the dry gulleys become rushing torrents after a rare downpour and can literally turn a desert into a place of grass and flowers overnight.[20] This points to times of revival that are sudden and massive, the kind that historians write about. The second picture is in verses

5–6, "farming at its most heartbreaking," a long and arduous process when the weather is bad and the soil is hard. The image is one of those who, in the absence of rain, still get a harvest through steady, faithful work, watering the ground with their tears if they have no other source of water. It depicts gospel workers who spend years of hard work, often weeping over the hardness of hearts that they see, and who bear little initial fruit.

And yet the psalmist is absolutely certain of eventual harvest— "God's blessing of seed sown and His visiting of His people." This is the final note. Kidner says that the modern translations tend to omit the extra words of emphasis in the final verb and therefore miss the psalmist's pointedness. No matter how long we may wait, neverthe- less "he that surely goes forth weeping ... will surely come home with shouts of joy."[21] Kidner concludes, "So the psalm, speaking first to its own times, speaks still. Miracles of the past it bids us treat as measures of the future; dry places as potential rivers; hard soil and good seed as the certain prelude to harvest."[22]

DISCUSSION QUESTIONS

1. Keller writes, "Maintenance prayer meetings are short, mechani- cal, and focused on physical needs inside the church. In contrast, the three basic traits of frontline prayer are these: a request for grace to confess sins and to humble ourselves; a compassion and zeal for the flourishing of the church and the reaching of the lost; and a yearning to know God, to see his face, to glimpse his glory." How have you experienced God working through "front- line" prayer? If you do not currently have these prayer times in your church, how can you go about beginning them?

2. One way to engage in gospel application is by training lay leaders to minister the gospel to others. This involves personal meetings and counseling to help people learn how to repent of their idols and self-righteousness. Does this type of gospel application currently happen in your church? If not, how can you begin training people to apply the gospel? How is ministering the gospel different from other forms of counseling?

3. Gospel innovation involves creatively communicating the gospel in new ways. How have you seen an overreliance on a particular communication style or methodology hinder a ministry? Why is it necessary to be innovative? What are some dangers associated with this?

4. The section titled "Preaching for Gospel Renewal" gives five characteristics that define preaching that leads to renewal. Which of these five do you need to strengthen? How can you incorporate these missing emphases into your preaching?

REFLECTIONS ON GOSPEL RENEWAL

Dane Ortlund, senior vice president at Crossway

The chapters on gospel renewal are among Tim Keller's most distinctive contribution to the church today. I suspect that those who are aware of only one or two emphases of Keller's ministry will find those here. It's in these chapters that we hear of three ways to live: religion versus the gospel, idolatry as a matter of gospel deficit, and preaching the whole Bible as testifying to Jesus.

I'd like to interact with this content from a few different angles. My hope is to advance the conversation, in gratitude to Tim Keller for the contribution he has made to the church in our time. This essay will be neither heavy on praise nor heavy on criticism, but rather will be an extended reflection as we all continue to strengthen what God is doing among us.

The distinctive articulations we find here have seeped into the evangelical consciousness with remarkable pervasiveness. While Keller has said many times that his formulations have been forged in and for the specific context of New York City (see, e.g., p. 141), what he says in these three chapters on gospel renewal transcends that specific urban niche. Doubtless this is partly due to what he rightly insists on in these chapters—that works-righteousness is "the default mode of the *human heart*" (p. 116, emphasis mine). If this is the case, then it is not only New Yorkers who need to see the distinction between religion and the gospel. Cultural Christians from

Alabama need to hear this, as do ranchers in Montana, academics in Boston, actors in Los Angeles, musicians in Nashville, and—as I discovered—seminary students in the Midwest. It was while studying at Covenant Seminary in St. Louis that I became familiar with Keller's ministry after being assigned an article or two of his to read. Soon after, my dad introduced me to Keller's preaching, and I was given fresh language and categories to make sense of not only the Bible's theology of spirituality but also my own experience.

These three chapters in *Shaped by the Gospel* touch a nerve common to all fallen human beings (the subtle instinct to strengthen our standing before God with obedience), and the content of these chapters has given large swaths of Protestantism categories through which to communicate the gospel to unbelievers and also to grow in the freedom of grace as believers. And we ought not to limit the impact of these truths to North America—as evident, for example, through the global Redeemer City to City initiative.

Let's begin, then, with two contributions Tim Keller has made to the church in our generation. We'll then move to two areas in which I think the conversation can be fruitfully advanced by filling out his teaching in the Gospel Renewal section of his book.

Three Ways to Live

Particularly helpful in the chapters on gospel renewal is Keller's understanding of the psychology of fallen human moral existence and how the gospel heals us. One way he gets at this is by explaining three ways to live: irreligion, religion, and gospel (p. 114).

This articulation crisply clarifies that there are two ways to reject God, not one—not only by selfish disobedience but also by selfish obedience. There is a deep, dark sickness festering within every man and woman, a strange psychosis that resists the freeness of God's favor. Though I am not using the label "psychosis" in a clinical way, I do mean it literally: the dictionary defines *psychosis* as "a very serious mental illness that makes you behave strangely or believe things that are not true." That is precisely our problem. Left to ourselves, we *cannot* receive grace-based acceptance. We stubbornly insist that we must contribute to our standing before God. A merit-based relationship with God is not something we occasionally slip into at times; it is how we all, more than we realize, constantly function. When Keller refers to works righteousness as our default mode, he is not identifying something common to a few Pharisees. He is identifying something that plagues all of humanity. No one escapes this. It is the water we all swim in. It feels normal to us.

Articulating *three* ways to live, rather than two, makes it more difficult to blindly mistake outward virtue for true godliness. If it is possible to do the right thing out of a wrong heart, then what matters most is not what we do but why we do it. The key thing is not the action externally but the motive internally. What matters is the state of the *heart*—which Keller rightly explains is, according to the Bible, not just our emotions but the animating engine to all we do and feel (p. 108). This triad enables unbelievers to see that we are not simply inviting them to clean up their lives for Jesus. We are not inviting the irreligious to become religious, but rather to receive the gospel of grace, the gospel that insists we lay down both our bad and our good to be embraced freely by God.

This focus on three ways to live reminds us that justification is outside-in, coming to us as an alien righteousness. And sanctification is inside-out, as we are transformed on the inside, and it manifests itself on the outside in good works of love. The "religious" mode of living wrongly reverses each of these. Religion treats justification as inside-out (personal holiness generates a right status) and sanctification as outside-in (right behavior necessarily reflects a right heart). In both cases the gospel is neglected.

By highlighting the three ways to live, Keller has helped our generation see the slipperiness of our hearts, our evasiveness when it comes to grace. This teaching makes sense of our hearts. We as fallen people are so complex and our hearts so unsearchable that we will even make our understanding of grace another form of evading it—as, for example, in dead orthodoxy, where gospel truth is defended but without vitality. We can unsay with our tone what we say with our lips. *How* we say what we believe tells us what we really believe. I was certainly guilty of this early on in my seminary days, and I cringe to reflect on how I used to commend the doctrines of grace in an ungracious way. It is not hard to find this today—blogs and blog comments come immediately to mind.

When we see that religion is just as morally bankrupt before God as irreligion (the only difference being that the religious are not aware of their bankruptcy), we can stop eluding true grace and let ourselves be loved by God *in* our mess rather than only after we get better. This threefold way of understanding Christianity brings clarity about the gospel as distinct from religion and is particularly needed in the wake of the Christian Right, the Moral Majority, and the cultural Christianity of the latter decades of the twentieth century, a time when the gospel and religion were easily confused.

It is intriguing to discover that this articulation of three ways to live also has some historical pedigree. Keller himself credits several writers with helping him come to this formulation, such as C. S. Lewis in his short essay "Three Kinds of Men."[1] Lewis comes close to this triad in his essay "Man or Rabbit?" and its statement that two kinds of human sin need healing—both "the worried, conscientious, ethical" kind of sin (religion) and "the cowardly and sensual" kind (irreligion).[2] Keller also frequently quotes from Richard Lovelace, drawing especially on Lovelace's insight that fallen humans tend to base their justification on their sanctification rather than their sanctification on their justification.[3]

I have enjoyed discovering a similar triad in other thinkers from the past. Martin Luther, for example, preached a sermon in 1521 titled "The Three Kinds of Good Life for the Instruction of Consciences." The point of his sermon is that we can approach morality out of three basic mind-sets. The first is the mind-set of those who are "hardened and blind"[4] (equivalent to what Keller labels "irreligion"). Others, though, may have a well-developed conscience, aware of the need for "humility, meekness, gentleness, peace, fidelity, love, propriety, purity, and the like."[5] Yet these can go wrong when they obey only because they "fear disgrace, punishment, or hell ... And this false ground is so deep that no saint has ever fathomed its bottom."[6] (This is what Keller calls "religion.") It is doing the right thing from a wrong motive. The third option is to obey God "gladly and willingly," Luther writes, out of "a pure, free, cheerful, glad, and loving heart, a heart which is simply gratuitously righteous, seeking no reward, fearing no punishment."[7] This third approach is an inside-out sanctification that is based on an outside-in justification, and it is the formula Keller presents for gospel renewal.

Others have also expressed a threefold way of understanding obedience. Søren Kierkegaard referred to three categories of moral existence: aesthetic, ethical, and religious. The aesthetic lives selfishly for one's own pleasure ("irreligion"). The ethical lives reluctantly in accordance with an external moral norm ("religion"). To be religious, however (used positively in Kierkegaard's terms), means to live in the glad abandon of faith (what Keller defines as "gospel" over against "religion").[8] F. B. Meyer, the English Baptist pastor a century ago, similarly wrote, "There are three kinds of men. First, those who have no intention. Second, those who have a double intention. Third, those whose intention is pure and simple."[9] One can also find this threefold way to live the Christian life in Thomas Aquinas,[10] Blaise Pascal,[11] Jonathan Edwards,[12] Herman Ridderbos,[13] and Karl Barth.[14]

While the notion of two ways to reject God has some historical precedence, no one appears to have given it the crisp and compelling articulation that we find in *Center Church* and Tim Keller's ministry as a whole. Indeed, the categories and language used to express this are so clear and helpful that younger church leaders must pay special care to avoid simply parroting Keller and the way he puts things. They must find their own fresh way of casting these biblical truths, building on our rich historical tradition.

Preaching Christ from Every Text

A second area of agreement and appreciation is Keller's focus on preaching, and especially a certain kind of preaching. This comes largely in chapter 6 titled "The Work of Gospel Renewal."

Keller begins by reminding us that the whole Bible is basically about one Person, Jesus Christ. The Bible is not a collection of diverse narratives about many different exemplary humans. Jesus is not only the most important figure in Scripture; he is the light that illumines it all, the key that unlocks it all, the climax and the organizing principle. He is the *point*. Keller's homiletical approach here is supported today by a host of younger preachers, as well as several peers such as Bryan Chapell, Sidney Greidanus, Edmund Clowney, Graeme Goldsworthy, and D. A. Carson. This christocentric hermeneutic is, I would argue, what Jesus himself demands, given what we find in passages such as John 5:39–47 or Luke 24:27, 44. This hermeneutic is not an imbalanced Trinitarianism, moreover, because the Father and the Spirit themselves are eager to spotlight Christ (John 8:54; 15:26).[15]

Alongside this Christ-centeredness in Keller's preaching strategy is a grace-centeredness. The basic message of the Bible is God's grace to sinners. As J. Greshem Machen put it, "The very center and core of the whole Bible is the doctrine of the grace of God — the grace of God which depends not one whit upon anything that is in man, but is absolutely undeserved."[16]

At times this grace-centered method of preaching has been challenged on the charge that preachers ought not to simply preach the gospel but rather the whole counsel of God (of which the gospel of grace is but one dimension). Yet we should note that the very passage from which we get the phrase "the whole counsel of God" (Acts 20:27 ESV) sets this phrase in parallel to "the gospel of the grace of God" (Acts 20:24 ESV). In both cases Paul is summarizing the teaching content of his ministry. This merits reflection and leads me to conclude that "the whole counsel of God," in biblical context, does not mean "preach the gospel of grace plus a bunch of other things, and don't forget those other things." Instead, it means something more like "preach the gospel of grace, as this gospel causes every aspect of life to flower into health and vitality, whether eldership or missionary endeavors or suffering or doctrine or ..." This seems a fitting interpretation in light of how Paul brings the gospel to bear on all kinds of issues throughout his letters, from the final judgment (Rom 2:16) to Gentile inclusion (Rom 11:28) to pastors' salaries (1 Cor 9:12) to future resurrection (1 Cor 15:3–5) to financial generosity (2 Cor 9:8) to table fellowship (Gal 2:14) to daily work (1 Thess 2:9).

Tim Keller emphasizes preaching as the primary means of nurturing gospel renewal. This needs to be stressed today as varieties of Christian activity proliferate. Amid the flood of counsel washing into our lives, from Twitter feeds to Oprah to our accountants, preaching remains God's primary established channel for gospel renewal. Many voices in Christian leadership are calling for a shifting from monological discourse to more dialogical and conversational preaching. Yet while there is room for a variety of homiletical approaches to reach different peoples and cultures, Keller reminds us that the New Testament calls for a heralding of good news, the trumpeting of an announcement, that transcends cultural locatedness.

Union with Christ

I'd like to turn now to ask two questions of these gospel renewal chapters, raising a few matters we should bear in mind as we appropriate this excellent content on gospel renewal. The first has to do with the New Testament's teaching on union with Christ.

These chapters present an insightful portrait of how the gospel fuels godly living by "melting" rather than "bending" the heart (pp. 121–22). We are reminded of the way Paul motivates the Corinthians toward financial generosity (for example) by fixing their minds on what Jesus did in his gracious work of gospel substitution (p. 123). This is rich and profound in explaining the psychological dynamic of living by grace. Yet I would welcome further reflection from Keller and others as to how the emphases of *Center Church* intersect with the doctrine of union with Christ, which may provide an even deeper reality in which Paul grounds Christian discipleship and renewal.[17] Union with Christ is the bedrock of Christian salvation, the most fundamental truth. As John Calvin put it, "We must understand that as long as Christ remains outside of us, and we are separated from him, all that he has suffered and done for the salvation of the human race remains useless."[18]

A test case here is the famous passage that bridges the end of Romans 5 into Romans 6. Paul spends five chapters diagnosing universal human guilt and the utter gratuity of grace on account of the work of Christ, concluding that no amount of law breaking can threaten our righteous standing before God. On the contrary, "where sin increased, grace abounded all the more" (Rom. 5:20 ESV). God's grace ever outruns our failures. This prompts the natural question that Paul asks: Why shouldn't we sin all the more to make grace increase?

What is Paul's answer? Keller's chapters on gospel renewal might lead us to expect the answer, "By no means! Consider the

gospel, until it melts your heart and moves you to holiness of life."
Yet Paul writes:

> By no means! How can we who died to sin still live in
> it? Do you not know that all of us who have been baptized
> into Christ Jesus were baptized into his death? We were buried
> therefore with him by baptism into death, in order that, just as
> Christ was raised from the dead by the glory of the Father, we
> too might walk in newness of life.
> For if we have been united with him in a death like his,
> we shall certainly be united with him in a resurrection like his.
>
> *Romans 6:2–5 ESV*

When tackling the question of whether the gospel is a license to
sin, Paul does not drive home pardoning grace all the more. Rather,
he places the gospel in the broader reality of a believer having been
united to Christ. Union with Christ is central throughout these
key chapters on sanctification (Rom 6–8). Repeatedly throughout
his letters Paul grounds Christian living in union with Christ.
Writing to young people, the Princeton theologian Charles Hodge
(1797–1878) remarked, "The doctrine of sanctification, therefore,
as taught in the Bible is, that we are made holy not by the force of
conscience, nor of moral motives, nor by acts of discipline, but by
being united to Christ."[19]

It is perhaps not immediately obvious what Paul has in mind
in these texts when he speaks of being united to Christ, but New
Testament scholarship sees two basic dimensions to it, which we
could call micro and macro, or vital and federal.[20] At a micro level,
to be united to Christ is the most intimate of associations. It is a vital
union of which sexual union is the faintest image and pointer—as
evidenced in Paul's argument in 1 Corinthians 6, where the apostle
motivates Christians not to be united to a prostitute sexually because

they are united to Christ spiritually. As in Romans 6, Paul does not root his ethical motivation in the freeness of grace so much as in the believer's union with Christ.

And at a macro level, to be "in Christ" is set opposite to being "in Adam." Everyone belongs to one realm or the other, under one representative ("federal") leader or the other. The key to making sense of this contrast between being in Adam or in Christ is inaugurated eschatology. Christ launched the end-time, longed-for new age in the middle of history; when we are saved, we are transferred from the old age of Adam into the new age of Christ, even though remnants of the old age still cling to us (thus the language of living in "the overlap of the ages"). This macro way of speaking of union with Christ is also used in the New Testament to fuel gospel renewal and fresh obedience (e.g., Col 3:1–11).[21]

Tim Keller's broader ministry reflects a rich understanding of all this. I am only asking whether, in light of the way the New Testament explains spiritual growth, these chapters ought to integrate union with Christ more explicitly into the vision of gospel renewal. In chapter 5, "The Essence of Gospel Renewal," several passages are brought forth to address the question of "how the Bible calls us to change" (pp. 123–25). I want to affirm the basic point Keller makes here—namely, that a major way the New Testament fuels growth is by calling us to enjoy the grace that is freely ours, rather than trying to crowbar our behavior into a certain shape. Yet even the passages cited by Keller place their motivation for change in the broader context of union with Christ. In Ephesians 5, the husband is indeed called on to love his wife, "just as Christ loved the church and gave himself up for her" (Eph 5:25)—a gospel motivation, to be sure. Yet Paul then goes on to speak at even greater length of the fact that we are to love our wives in light of our union with Christ, of which the marital union is a glimmer and echo (5:28–32).[22]

The point in all this is not fundamental disagreement with

Keller's formulation of the power of the gospel to generate true heart-change. But I do think this formulation should be more broadly placed within a framework of union with Christ.[23] One might question the degree to which this doctrine will compute with unbelievers, whether in New York City or anywhere else. Surely speaking in terms of forgiveness and acquittal is more readily understandable, especially in our highly litigious society. Yet while union with Christ is perhaps less concrete, we can communicate this truth in terms that make it come alive in unbelieving hearts, as Keller so winsomely does. We can speak, for example, of the existential sense of being "cut off"—of being broken off, fractured, separated, *out*. As Tolkien put it in a 1945 letter to his son, "Certainly there was an Eden on this very unhappy earth. We all long for it, and we are constantly glimpsing it: our whole nature at its best and least corrupted, its gentlest and most humane, is still soaked with the sense of 'exile.'"[24] The reconnection with our true self, our restoration to that from which we have been exiled, is found in the union, both vitally and federally, of a fallen human being with Christ.

It is wonderful when the reality of one's union to the living Christ comes home. I remember sitting in Phil Douglass's spiritual formation class at Covenant Seminary in the fall of 2002 and hearing for the first time of the macro-significance of being united to Christ. The gracious inevitability of my final deliverance from sin came home in a fresh and powerful way. I thought, *I cannot sin myself out of my union with him.* I have been irreversibly joined to the resurrected Lord. Nothing is left to chance. Countless times in the years between then and now, my union with Christ has strengthened me to say no to sin when tempted and calmed me back into sanity the many times I have given in to temptation.

The Heart of Christ

One other matter may be worth raising in an effort to fill out the teaching of these chapters on gospel renewal. I wonder if, in the highly illuminating articulation of the gospel in these chapters, the actual person of Christ is in danger of being quietly backgrounded, and the ceiling thus lowered on the potential for gospel renewal. Are the wonderfully clear formulations of these chapters a bit cerebral, or formulaic? Too heavy on the transactional nature of salvation and too light on the personal nature of salvation?

Let me put it this way. Is it possible to be gospel-centered to the neglect of being Christ-centered? In the categories of systematic theology, might we focus on the work of Christ to the exclusion of the person of Christ? Could we at times be in danger of becoming gospel-centrality-centered instead of gospel-centered in a way that fixes our eyes on Christ?[25]

To be sure, what we find in these chapters is crystal clear on the gospel of grace. And no one can say everything any time he says anything! Moreover, we do at a few points in these chapters find Christ himself held forth, such as in the discussion of making the truth not only clear but also real (p. 138). But I wonder if readers of this content on gospel renewal will need to be extra careful not to unwittingly neglect Jesus himself. The consistent drumbeat of "faith in the gospel" (p. 126) is wise and right. The glorious objectivity of the gospel of grace shines through with sparkling clarity. But we should not allow this gospel focus to become detached from Christ himself.

One angle that could prove especially rich in this regard is reflection on the heart of Christ. Spurgeon pointed out once that in the one place in all four Gospels where Jesus tells us about his heart, Jesus says it is "gentle and lowly" (Matt 11:29 ESV).[26] And this heart of Christ, given to us by word in Matthew 11, is given to us by deed over and over again in the Gospels. Throughout his ministry, Jesus draws near to the messy, the despairing, the sorrowful, and he stiff-arms the proud, the elite, the "clean." We see him sweeping the children up into his arms (Mark 10:16), weeping at the death of Lazarus (John 11:35), and deeply distraught at the grief of his friends in the face of death (John 11:33). This is a man of profound feeling.

My point is that as weary sinners walk into our churches on the weekend, gospel renewal will be fueled not only by the light of clear gospel articulations but also by the heat of warm depictions of who Jesus himself is. Hearts are renewed as they relax into the happy calm of knowing that it is in their fickle messiness, not once they get beyond it, that the heart of Christ is drawn out to them and is *for* them — that he is the friend of sinners (Matt 11:19). The objectivity of gospel truth must be wedded with the subjectivity of Jesus' heart. Sinners must bathe in reminders that Christ not only satisfied justice but also is drawn irresistibly toward despairing failures. God yearns for his wandering people (Jer 31:20).

Without objective gospel truth, of course, the heart of Christ will be impossible to enjoy. We must know that our record is clean, that all guilt has been removed, that we stand complete in the finished work of Christ. But this objective truth is not the endpoint, it seems to me, but the channel by which sinners — present sinners, not just past ones — can feel embraced by an actual Person, the Friend of failures. We exercise faith in Christ, not faith in the gospel.[27]

This more subjective dimension was integral to the effectiveness of the great revivalists of the eighteenth century. George Whitefield, the Wesleys, and Jonathan Edwards spoke of *Christ* just as much as (or more than) the *gospel*. My own mind has been shaped most deeply at this point by the Puritans, especially in books like John Owen's *Communion with the Triune God* ("there is not the meanest, the weakest, the poorest believer on the earth, but Christ prizes him more than all the world besides"[28]) and Thomas Goodwin's *The*

Heart of Christ ("how his heart beats and his affections yearn toward us, even now he is in glory"[29]).

Perhaps this emphasis on the heart of Christ, complementing the wonderful recovery of a clear gospel formula, is what will prevent young preachers who discover the gospel afresh from veering off into antinomianism. If it is true not only that a transaction has taken place and I am now counted righteous before God, but also that I now enjoy a living communion with a Person, then while my sins need not count against me, my sins do indeed hinder fellowship with this Person. In his book *Holiness by Grace*, Bryan Chapell shows that while some things cannot change in our walk with God, other things can. What cannot change are our sonship, God's desire for our welfare, his affection for us, his love for us, our eternal destiny, and our final security. But what *can* change are our felt fellowship with God, our experience of his blessing, our assurance of his love, his delight in our actions, his discipline, and our sense of guilt.[30]

This distinction between what is static versus what is dynamic in our walk with God protects the invincible gratuity of the gospel (which comes through loud and clear in *Center Church*), while making room for the inescapable biblical teaching on how our enjoyment of God does vacillate according to our obedience and disobedience. Reflection on the heart of Christ helps us to take into account this more subjective, relational, person-to-Person aspect of the Christian life, complementing the doctrines of grace with the Man of grace.

Conclusion

It would be difficult to overstate the clarity and insight of what we find in these chapters on gospel renewal. Even the reflections above on union with Christ and the heart of Christ are not contradictory to Tim Keller's teaching but rather intended to further fill it out. Any church, and any believer, who prayerfully takes this book and seeks by grace to integrate it into their lives will be building on a rocky, not a sandy, foundation (Matt 7:24–28).

As I have indicated already, it is particularly the younger generation I have had in mind when identifying ways to fill out the teaching of *Center Church*. Tim Keller has been granted an unusually wide-ranging and profound influence, especially among my generation (I am thirty-five at the time of writing this). Those whose eyes have been opened to the wonder of the gospel through Keller's teaching must be extra vigilant to receive all that the Bible says about the Christian life and personal renewal, lest their appropriate enthusiasm over Keller's articulations become parroted regurgitations. They must find their own way of stating gospel truths in their own contexts through their own personalities.

And yet it is easy for me to conclude by affirming that there is perhaps no other comparable piece of contemporary writing to which I would send anyone who is stuck in their Christian discipleship or who is wanting to know more about the core dynamic of living the Christian life before *Center Church*.[31]

RESPONSE TO DANE ORTLUND

Timothy Keller

Grateful

It was an encouragement and a surprise to hear Dane Ortlund's claim that the teaching on gospel renewal in this section of *Shaped by the Gospel* has "seeped into the evangelical consciousness" (p. 151) and has had an effect particularly on a younger (than me) generation of ministers and leaders. If this is true, I'm gratified, to say the least, but also humbled. And I'm not just saying "humbled" because we're supposed to say that in these kinds of interchanges.

On this subject of renewal and revival, I see myself as bringing out, fairly intact, the wisdom of older times regarding this subject in the writings of men, especially Jonathan Edwards. It feels strange to get much credit for this material. It seems to be simply a popularization of the work of older masters. But whatever the causes may be for people giving this a hearing, I'm grateful.

I was also glad for Ortlund's enrichment of the "Three Ways" model (pp. 152–56). Ultimately, this is nothing more than the classic distinctions between legalism, antinomianism, and the gospel. But he has discovered this "triad" described and expounded in imaginative ways also in the work of Martin Luther, Søren Kierkegaard, F. B. Meyer, Thomas Aquinas, Blaise Pascal, Herman Ridderbos, and Karl Barth. I was aware of some of these but not others, and

I'm delighted to be able to follow his citations and deepen my own understanding of how to present these three ways to listeners so that the gospel alternative is clearer in their minds.

Helpful

One of Ortlund's two gracious critiques (which he kindly calls "proposals for moving the conversation forward") is that the discussion in these chapters could lead us to be "clear on the gospel of grace" but without "Christ himself held forth." He wonders if "readers of this content on gospel renewal will need to be extra careful not to unwittingly neglect Jesus himself" (p. 162). He thinks that in this section "the glorious objectivity of the gospel of grace" is sparklingly clear, but there is not as much emphasis on Jesus himself. Others have described this as offering listeners the benefits of Christ's salvation without offering them Christ. Does the Gospel Renewal material make this mistake?

Earlier in his essay, Ortlund expresses agreement and appreciation for my thesis that one primary means to gospel renewal is to preach Christ from every text, to show within every sermon how the particular content and themes of the scriptural passage point to and find their fulfillment and climax in Christ. He then writes, "Alongside this Christ-centeredness in Keller's preaching strategy is a grace-centeredness" (p. 156). I would generally not put it that way. To be Christ-centered in preaching should be the way to be grace-centered. A text expounded without being tied to Christ's person and work will be implicitly or explicitly a moralistic exhortation. Following the biblical theme of the passage through to Christ can embed the imperatives of the text within the indicatives of the saving work of Christ. And that is how to preach a grace-centered message.

We should add a caveat here. I have heard sermons that were

ostensibly Christ-centered in that they spoke a lot about him, yet in the end held him up more as an example, or inspiration, or even as the "climax of our biblical theme"—but his saving benefits to us were not made clear. What we are looking for is what John Calvin spoke of: "This, then, is the true knowledge of Christ, if we receive him as he is offered by the Father: namely, clothed with his gospel."[1]

That great phrase "Christ ... clothed with his gospel" expresses what every preacher should be presenting to his listeners. Not an abstract offer of pardon or even simply a sermon that points to Christ as being admirable in various ways. It is to *lift up Christ himself,* full of all the benefits of his salvation for those who unite with him by faith.

Now, Ortlund feels that the material in these chapters does not make this crystal clear. Despite the brief section on Christ-centered preaching, the reader could get the impression that you could talk of the objective benefits but "neglect Jesus himself." If that is true—and it may be—then Ortlund is rightly sensing a missing piece in the gospel renewal chapters. Originally, I was going to include in this part of *Center Church* a full chapter on preaching Christ for gospel renewal. But as I wrote it, it became too long to be a single chapter, and then for even inclusion in the book at all. It was determined that I should produce a separate book, which was recently published as *Preaching: Communicating Faith in an Age of Skepticism* (New York: Viking, 2015). What I say about preaching Christ in *Center Church* is quite brief—too brief to overcome Ortlund's concern. And so it may be that readers and learners will need to read *Center Church* along with my book on preaching to avoid the mistakes against which he warns.

Intriguing

The other of Dane Ortlund's gracious criticisms has to do with "union with Christ." He notes that in the gospel renewal material, the primary motivation for godliness and holiness put forth is that of gratitude for gracious salvation. Paul, for example, in 2 Corinthians 8:9, motivates financial generosity through pointing listeners not only to Jesus' substitutionary death ("though he was rich, yet for your sake he became poor") but also to our new standing before God due to his work ("so that you through his poverty might become rich"). Because we are rich with spiritual wealth that we did not earn, we, too, should be generous with our goods, even to the point of sacrifice. Ortlund agrees this is sanctification being motivated by gratitude for substitutionary atonement and justification. "This is rich and profound in explaining the psychological dynamic of living by grace," writes Ortlund (p. 158).

However, Ortlund then asks why the gospel renewal material does not also motivate holiness the way Paul does in Romans 6, where he appeals not to our pardon and justification or to Jesus' substitutionary work, but to our "union with Christ." He also points out that in 1 Corinthians 6, Paul motivates Christians to avoid sexual immorality because we are united to Christ. Ortlund knows that elsewhere I use these motivations in my preaching. He just wishes that in the material about how to renew people with the gospel, I had brought in union with Christ as well, which he thinks "may provide an even deeper reality in which Paul grounds Christian discipleship and renewal" than does "fixing the mind on Jesus' gracious work of gospel substitution" (p. 158).

I would not agree that union with Christ is a "deeper reality" than gospel grace, or that consciousness of union with Christ is a deeper motivation than gratitude for gracious salvation. The gospel is that sinners are saved by Christ's work, not by our work. That means Jesus' "gracious work of gospel substitution" does not secure only pardon and justification by sheer grace, but also *everything else*—adoption, the indwelling Holy Spirit, a new name or identity, fellowship and access through prayer, and union with him.

What lies behind the statement that union is "a deeper reality" is the truth that in some ways, "union with Christ" is not simply one more of the benefits of salvation but it is that which holds the rest together. There is a sense in which each of the benefits is simply an aspect of our union with Christ. Justification is our forensic or legal union with him, so that now Christ's righteousness becomes ours. Regeneration and the indwelling of the Spirit are aspects of our vital, or spiritual, union with him. Adoption, identity change, and prayer reflect the personal union of love we have with him. Our membership in the body of Christ means we are brought into union with all those who are united to Christ. So being united with Christ is a crucial biblical concept that holds all these other benefits together. It prevents us from seeing them as discrete things that are dispensed to us if we do this or that. Becoming a Christian is being "in Christ"—a shorthand way of saying that we have received all these benefits by Christ's work when we receive him. So when preachers call listeners to "enjoy the grace that is freely ours," they do not need to say, "But also you are united to Christ." Being united to Christ is by *his* work, not ours, and so it is not a different reality but is part of the grace that we are enjoying.

I will leave to one side the current theological controversy behind this topic. That controversy is occupied with questions about the relationship of justification, sanctification, and union. While that debate isn't irrelevant to this discussion, our main concern is whether the doctrine of union with Christ is a way to motivate and renew people with the gospel, and whether I have neglected it somewhat, not in my own ministry and preaching, but in these pages.

My first response (there is a second!) is that the neglect of union with Christ in these chapters is more apparent than real. As Ortlund points out, it is not easy for preachers to preach on union with Christ, which at first sight is a "less concrete" concept. He then gives an example of one way to do it, namely, by talking about exile and the sense that we are cut off from our true home. That is indeed a fruitful way to do it.

Perhaps the main way of talking about union with Christ, especially in the Romans 6 passage cited by Ortlund, is that of a transfer from one "realm"—field of influence and power—to another, and from being under one master or lord to being under a new one. Doug Moo, in his masterful treatment of Romans 5 and 6, speaks about two realms—one of sin and death; one of righteousness and life. Each realm has a founding "act"—the disobedience of Adam and the obedience of Christ. Union with Christ happens when we are transferred from one realm, where we have been mastered by sin and death, to the realm of Christ. We were slaves in the old realm, but in the new realm we have freedom.[2] The reason it should be unthinkable for a Christian to sin is that we have been given to a new master: "You are not your own; you were bought at a price" (1 Cor 6:19–20). We should not sin, because we no longer have to—we've been freed from its dominion. And we should not sin, because it would be a trampling on the work of the one who gave up everything to set us free.

So how do you preach about this without having it sound like a lot of remote theology to most listeners? One of the primary ways to get at the "realm transfer" teaching is to preach about sin in the form of idolatry—of having other "masters" besides God. Part of the Gospel Renewal material is devoted to this. Luther showed us that when the Bible declares that we are to have no other gods before God (Exod 20:2), and that we are to be justified by faith alone, not by our works (Gal 2:16), it is saying essentially the same thing. The way we try to justify ourselves, achieve our own honor and self-worth, craft an identity—without God—is by making created things into pseudo-saviors and gods. And the way to break the power of those masters over us is to say, "But Jesus has achieved for you, by grace, all the things you wrongly look for from those things." When we slide back into idolatry, we do so because we forget where our true justification lies and who our true love and Savior is. We must look to him and who we are and what we have in him in order to say to our idols, "You cannot rule my life anymore." This is a way to preach the basic principle of Romans 6—that we are free from sin, yet we must not go back into it because we belong to Jesus and are united to him.

Now it is important to realize that we preachers don't have to use the metaphor of "idolatry" every time to get across this crucial truth that we must not let sin continue to rule over us. Augustine talks about "disordered loves"—loving God too little and other things too much. Søren Kierkegaard talks about "false identities"—building a self on something besides God. There are many ways to convey, even to very secular people, the basic idea of slavery to sin and freedom through Christ's saving benefits.

The concept of idolatry is a way of preaching gospel grace by using the Romans 6 definition of sin as slavery and of salvation as freedom, as expressions of our union with Christ. Therefore the gospel renewal material, I think, escapes reducing the gospel to just freedom from guilt or reducing motivation to simply thankfulness from pardon.

Having said that, my second response to Ortlund's critique is that he is right in saying I should make clearer the connections of gospel renewal to union with Christ. And I think it is fair to say that here, too, these connections would be much clearer if we connected the teaching of gospel renewal dynamics with more thorough training in Christ-centered, expository preaching. If you preach through the Bible, you will constantly be getting to all the "facets" of gospel gratitude for grace. We are adopted; therefore we should pray to and resemble the Father (Matt 6:5–9; Eph 1:4–5). We are indwelt by the Holy Spirit; therefore we should not engage in unholy immorality (1 Cor 6:19). We bear his name now, and so we want to honor that name (Acts 5:41; 2 Tim 2:19). Our love makes us want to behold him by faith, and that changes us into his likeness (2 Cor 3:18). We should even fear Christ—have "reverence for" him (Eph 5:21). The "fear of God," even in the Old Testament, increased with an increasing grasp of grace (Ps 130:4). The concept of "fearing Christ," then, means we should live in joy-filled, trembling awe that one so holy and infinite should love us so sacrificially and wholly. So we obey him because we want to please him and resemble him, not dishonor or grieve him.

These motivations are different in many regards. But as John Owen points out in *Of the Mortification of Sin in Believers*, any motivation for holiness that is not rooted in a deep grasp of the fact that our salvation is a gift unachieved by us turns the effort at holiness into a spiritually deadly attempt to put God in our debt and earn our own salvation.[3] Such duties will not change our hearts but will only create external morality while the heart maintains a fatal self-sufficiency and rebellion. So at bottom, all of these different motivations, even the knowledge that I am united to Christ and thus should not sin, is a response to the grace of God.

I agree with Dane Ortlund that this rich complexity of biblical concepts and resources for gospel renewal is too implicit and not spelled out very well, and an awareness of this can give good guidance for enhancing future versions of this material.

ABBREVIATIONS

Bible Books

Gen	Genesis	Lam	Lamentations
Exod	Exodus	Ezek	Ezekiel
Lev	Leviticus	Dan	Daniel
Num	Numbers	Hos	Hosea
Deut	Deuteronomy	Joel	Joel
Josh	Joshua	Amos	Amos
Judg	Judges	Obad	Obadiah
Ruth	Ruth	Jonah	Jonah
1–2 Sam	1–2 Samuel	Mic	Micah
1–2 Kgs	1–2 Kings	Nah	Nahum
1–2 Chr	1–2 Chronicles	Hab	Habakkuk
Ezra	Ezra	Zeph	Zephaniah
Neh	Nehemiah	Hag	Haggai
Esth	Esther	Zech	Zechariah
Job	Job	Mal	Malachi
Ps/Pss	Psalm/Psalms	Matt	Matthew
Prov	Proverbs	Mark	Mark
Eccl	Ecclesiastes	Luke	Luke
Song	Song of Songs	John	John
Isa	Isaiah	Acts	Acts
Jer	Jeremiah	Rom	Romans

1–2 Cor	1–2 Corinthians	Phlm	Philemon
Gal	Galatians	Heb	Hebrews
Eph	Ephesians	Jas	James
Phil	Philippians	1–2 Pet	1–2 Peter
Col	Colossians	1–2–3 John	1–2–3 John
1–2 Thess	1–2 Thessalonians	Jude	Jude
1–2 Tim	1–2 Timothy	Rev	Revelation
Titus	Titus		

General

cf. . . . . *confer*, compare

ch(s). . . . . . . chapter(s)

ed(s). . . . . . . editor(s), edited by, edition

e.g. . . . . *exempli gratia*, for example

esp. . . . . especially

et al. . . . . *et alii*, and others

ff. . . . . and the following ones

ibid. . . . . *ibidem*, in the same place

idem. . . . . . . that which was mentioned before, same, as in same author

i.e. . . . . *id est*, that is

n. . . . . note

p(p). . . . . page(s)

rev. . . . . revised

trans. . . . . . . translator, translated by

v(v). . . . . verse(s)

NOTES

Series Introduction

1. Richard Lints, *The Fabric of Theology: A Prolegomenon to Evangelical Theology* (Grand Rapids: Eerdmans, 1993), 9.

2. Ibid., 82.

3. Ibid., 315.

4. Ibid., 316–17.

5. These three areas correspond roughly to Richard Lints's four theological vision factors in this way: (1) *Gospel* flows from how you read the Bible; (2) *City* flows from your reflections on culture; and (3) *Movement* flows from your understanding of tradition. Meanwhile, the fourth factor—your view of human rationality—influences your understanding of all three. It has an impact on how you evangelize non-Christians, how much common grace you see in a culture, and how institutional (or anti-institutional) you are in your thinking about ministry structure.

6. It can be argued that the Gospel axis is not like the other two. In the other two axes, the desired position is a midpoint, a balance between extremes. However, Sinclair Ferguson (in his lectures on the Marrow Controversy) and others have argued that the gospel is not at all a balance between two opposites but an entirely different thing. In fact, it can also be argued that legalism and antinomianism are not opposites but essentially the same thing—self-salvation—opposed to the gospel. So please note that putting the gospel between these two extremes is simply a visual shorthand.

Chapter 1: The Gospel Is Not Everything

1. Mark 1:1; Luke 2:10; 1 Corinthians 1:16–17; 15:1–11.

2. D. A. Carson, "What Is the Gospel?—Revisited," in *For the Fame of God's Name: Essays in Honor of John Piper*, ed. Sam Storms and Justin Taylor (Wheaton, IL: Crossway, 2010), 158.

3. The verb translated "passed" in 1 John 3:14 is *metabainō* in the Greek, which means to "cross over." In John 5:24, Jesus states, "Whoever hears my word

and believes him who sent me has eternal life and will not be judged but has *crossed over* [*metabainō*] from death to life." A parallel passage is Colossians 1:13, where it is said that Christ followers have been transferred from the dominion of darkness into the kingdom of the Son.

4. D. Martyn Lloyd-Jones, *Spiritual Depression: Its Causes and Cure* (Grand Rapids: Eerdmans, 1965), 34.

5. J. I. Packer, "Introductory Essay to John Owen's *Death of Death in the Death of Christ*," www.all-of-grace.org/pub/others/deathofdeath.html (accessed February 14, 2015).

6. J. I. Packer, *Knowing God* (Downers Grove, IL: InterVarsity, 1973), 171.

7. Francis Schaeffer, *The Mark of the Christian* (Downers Grove, IL: InterVarsity, 1977) 25. Cf. Timothy George and John Woodbridge, *The Mark of Jesus: Loving in a Way the World Can See* (Chicago: Moody, 2005).

8. See Carson, "What Is the Gospel?—Revisited," in *For the Fame of God's Name*, 158.

9. Having heard and read this in the words of other preachers, I have never been able to track down an actual place in Tertullian's writings where he says it. I think it may be apocryphal, but the principle is right.

10. J. Gresham Machen, *Christianity and Liberalism*, new ed. (Grand Rapids: Eerdmans, 2001), 99.

11. J. I. Packer, *In My Place Condemned He Stood: Celebrating the Glory of the Atonement* (Wheaton, IL: Crossway, 2007), 26–27.

12. Simon Gathercole, "The Gospel of Paul and the Gospel of the Kingdom," in *God's Power to Save*, ed. Chris Green (Leicester, UK: Inter-Varsity, 2006), 138–54.

13. D. A. Carson (*The Difficult Doctrine of the Love of God* [Wheaton, IL: Crossway, 2000], 39, 43) writes, "What we have, then, is a picture of God whose love, even in eternity past, even before the creation of anything, is other-oriented. This cannot be said (for instance) of Allah. Yet because the God of the Bible is one, this plurality-in-unity does not destroy his entirely appropriate self-focus as God ... There has *always* been an other-orientation to the love of God ... We are the friends of God by virtue of the intra-Trinitarian love of God that so worked out in the fullness of time that the plan of redemption, conceived in the mind of God in eternity past, has exploded into our space-time history at exactly the right moment."

14. See "The Dance of Creation," in Timothy Keller, *The Reason for God: Belief in an Age of Skepticism* (New York: Dutton, 2008), 225–26; "The Dance," in Timothy Keller, *Jesus the King: Understanding the Life and Death of the Son of God* (New York: Riverhead, 2013), 3–13.

15. From the poem "The Second Coming" (1920) by William Butler Yeats.

16. Emily Bobrow, "David Foster Wallace, in His Own Words" (taken from

his 2005 commencement address at Kenyon College), http://moreintelligentlife
.com/story/david-foster-wallace-in-his-own-words (accessed February 14, 2015).

17. See C. S. Lewis, *Christian Reflections* (Grand Rapids: Eerdmans, 1967),
167–76.

18. Vinoth Ramachandra, *The Scandal of Jesus* (Downers Grove, IL:
InterVarsity, 2001), 24.

19. Thanks to Michael Thate for this illustration.

20. Carson, "What Is the Gospel?—Revisited," in *For the Fame of God's
Name*, 158.

Chapter 2: The Gospel Is Not a Simple Thing

1. See Mark D. Thompson, *A Clear and Present Word: The Clarity
of Scripture* (New Studies in Biblical Theology 21; Downers Grove, IL:
InterVarsity, 2006).

2. See Paul Woodbridge, "'Kingdom of God' and 'Eternal Life' in the
Synoptic Gospels and John," in *God's Power to Save: One Gospel for a Complex
World?* ed. Chris Green (Nottingham, UK: Inter-Varsity, 2006).

3. Ibid., 72.

4. Ibid., 64.

5. Simon Gathercole, "The Gospel of Paul and the Gospel of the
Kingdom," in *God's Power to Save*, ed. Chris Green (Leicester, UK: Inter-Varsity,
2008), 138–54.

6. Thanks to Dr. John Thomas for helping to bridge the worlds of anthro-
pology, linguistics, and theology in this area.

7. In the previous chapter, I gave one example of how to mix the two
approaches in a single blended gospel presentation.

8. See D. A. Carson, "The Biblical Gospel," in *For Such a Time as This:
Perspectives on Evangelicalism, Past, Present and Future*, ed. Steve Brady and
Harold Rowdon (London: Evangelical Alliance, 1996), 80–81.

9. See D. A. Carson, "Systematic Theology and Biblical Theology," in *New
Dictionary of Biblical Theology*, ed. T. Desmond Alexander and Brian S. Rosner
(Downers Grove, IL: InterVarsity, 2000), 89–104, esp. 97–98. See also the
"Series Prefaces" to the New Studies in Biblical Theology series, where Carson
gives a third definition of biblical theology as "the delineation of a biblical theme
across all or part of the biblical corpora."

10. There is an interesting way the Greek translators of the Hebrew Bible
(the Septuagint) handle references to the garden, namely, Eden. In places like
Genesis 2:9, 15–16; 3:1, 8, 10, and in Ezekiel 31:8, the Greek word *paradeisos* is
used to translate as "Eden" or "garden." This word is used in Luke 23:43 when
Jesus says to the penitent criminal on the cross, "Today you will be with me in

paradise" (*en tō paradeisō*), as well as by Paul in 2 Corinthians 12:4, when Paul reports being caught up to paradise (*eis ton paradeison*), and by John in Revelation 2:7, when one "like a son of man" (1:13) says to those in the church of Ephesus, "To him who overcomes, I will give the right to eat from the tree of life, which is in the paradise of God" (*en tō paradeisō tou theou*).

11. See also Isaiah 40:9–11; Mark 1:14–15.

Chapter 3: The Gospel Affects Everything

1. D. A. Carson, "The Gospel of Jesus Christ (1 Corinthians 15:1–19)," *The Spurgeon Fellowship Journal* (Spring 2008): 10–11, www.thespurgeonfellow ship.org/Downloads/feature_Sp08.pdf (accessed January 5, 2012); see also Carson's chapter "What Is the Gospel?—Revisited," in *For the Fame of God's Name: Essays in Honor of John Piper*, ed. Sam Storms and Justin Taylor (Wheaton, IL: Crossway, 2010), 164–66, where he writes that "the gospel is not just for unbelievers but also for believers" and makes the biblical case.

2. Lesslie Newbigin, *The Gospel in a Pluralist Society* (Grand Rapids: Eerdmans, 1989), 38, italics in original.

3. Simon Gathercole, "The Gospel of Paul and the Gospel of the Kingdom," in *God's Power to Save*, ed. Chris Green (Nottingham, UK: Inter-Varsity, 2006), 138–54.

4. Edward Fisher, *The Marrow of Modern Divinity* (1645; repr., Fearn, Scotland: Christian Focus, 2009).

5. See Thomas Chalmers, "The Expulsive Power of a New Affection" (sermon; date unknown), www.theologynetwork.org/historical-theology/getting-stuck-in/the-expulsive-power-of-a-new-affection.htm (accessed February 14, 2015).

6. Miroslav Volf, *A Public Faith: How Followers of Christ Should Serve the Common Good* (Grand Rapids: Baker, 2011), 92.

7. Carson, "What Is the Gospel?—Revisited," in *For the Fame of God's Name*, 165.

Response to Michael Horton

1. John Calvin, *Institutes of the Christian Religion*, ed. John T. McNeill (Philadelphia: Westminster, 1960), 1:696–97.

Chapter 4: The Need for Gospel Renewal

1. I am going to use the terms *renewal* and *revival* interchangeably.

2. Richard F. Lovelace, *Dynamics of Spiritual Life: An Evangelical Theology of Renewal* (Downers Grove, IL: InterVarsity, 1979), 101.

3. See ibid., 212.

4. For a varied reading list on revival, see Thomas S. Kidd, *The Great Awakening: The Roots of Evangelical Christianity in America* (New Haven, CT: Yale University Press, 2007); Mark Noll, "The New Piety: The Conversion of the Wesleys," in *Turning Points: Decisive Moments in the History of Christianity* (Grand Rapids: Baker, 2001), 221–44; D. Martyn Lloyd-Jones, *Revival* (Wheaton, IL: Crossway, 1987); Iain H. Murray, *Revival and Revivalism: The Making and Marring of American Evangelicalism 1750–1858* (Carlisle, PA: Banner of Truth, 1994); C. Goen, ed., *The Works of Jonathan Edwards: The Great Awakening* (New Haven, CT: Yale University Press, 1972); Richard F. Lovelace, *Dynamics of Spiritual Life* (Downers Grove, IL: InterVarsity, 1979).

5. For a recent survey, see Collin Hansen and John Woodbridge, *A God-Sized Vision: Revival Stories That Stretch and Stir* (Grand Rapids: Zondervan, 2010).

6. William B. Sprague, *Lectures on Revivals of Religion* (1832; repr., Edinburgh: Banner of Truth, 1958), 25–60.

7. See Noll, "The New Piety," in *Turning Points*, 221–44.

8. In the last several years, many young evangelical leaders have adopted this same critique. They have read neo-Anabaptist thinkers such as Stanley Hauerwas and William Willimon; older Anabaptist thinkers such as John Howard Yoder; "new monastics" such as Shane Claiborne; "high church Calvinists" such as Michael Horton and Darryl Hart; Federal Vision leaders such as Douglas Wilson; and those who follow Lesslie Newbigin and N. T. Wright. As different as these thinkers and groups are, they all put much emphasis on liturgy, catechism, thick and deep community, and weekly observance of the Lord's Supper. Revivalist religion is critiqued as being "Gnostic" (not involving the body, not caring for the physical), as being individualistic, and as seeking to ground assurance in shifting subjective experience rather than in more solid community participation and tradition. The call is to look to the sacraments and church involvement for assurance rather than to personal experience.

9. Sprague warns against these "evils" of revivalism: "undervaluing divine institutions and divine truth" (p. 242), "certain things ... that are fitted to impair the dignity and lessen the influence of the ministerial office" (p. 247), "setting up false standards of Christian character" (p. 249), and "admitting persons to the communion with little or no probation" (p. 254). It is remarkable that many of these criticisms are similar to those of modern social historians, theologians, and young evangelical leaders.

10. See Archibald Alexander, *Thoughts on Religious Experience* (Edinburgh: Banner of Truth, 1978), 13–35.

11. See Mark Noll, *The Old Religion in a New World: The History of North American Christianity* (Grand Rapids: Eerdmans, 2001), 51.

12. For two classic explanations of how pluralistic culture forces everyone to choose their faith, see Peter L. Berger, *The Homeless Mind: Modernization and Consciousness* (New York: Vintage, 1974); Peter L. Berger, *The Heretical Imperative: Contemporary Possibilities of Religious Affirmation* (New York: Doubleday, 1980).

13. Philippians 3:3 reads, "we who are *the* circumcision ..." "Circumcision" here is particular, communicating distinguishment. There is debate over whether "faith in Christ" in verse 9 is to be understood as an objective genitive ("faith in Christ") or subjective genitive ("faith/faithfulness of Christ"), but this doesn't affect our point. The passage is about what marks our identity—what we do (works of the flesh) or what has been done for us in Christ.

14. Martin Luther, *Commentary on Galatians* (Lafayette, IN: Sovereign Grace, 2002), 103.

Chapter 5: The Essence of Gospel Renewal

1. Throughout this chapter and much of the book, I use "religion" as a synonym for moralism and legalism. Certainly we can refer to the "Christian religion," but I will use "religion" more negatively, as a heuristic device, and I have a couple of good reasons for doing so: (1) The New Testament uses two words for "religion" or "religious"—*thrēskeia* and *deisidaimonia*—which Luke and Paul only use negatively (Acts 25:19; 26:5; Col 2:18 [NIV, "worship"]). James uses *thrēskeia* positively once (Jas 1:27), but negatively in 1:26. Hebrews has a number of similar terms for works-religion as well. (2) Sometime people contrast "religion" with "relationship," as in "Christianity isn't a religion; it is a relationship." This isn't what I mean, and some make such a statement to mean Christianity requires only an inner love relationship with God, not obedience, holiness of life, life in community, and discipline. Dietrich Bonhoeffer (*The Cost of Discipleship* [New York: Touchstone, 1995], 44–45) calls this "cheap grace"—the love of a non-holy God who didn't require costly atonement in order to reconcile us and whose love, therefore, does not require or provoke life change. The gospel is distinct from both cheap grace and religion.

2. The truth is that even seemingly irreligious people are actually religious. See the quote from David Foster Wallace referenced in chapter 1 (p. 34; Emily Bobrow, "David Foster Wallace, in His Own Words" [taken from his 2005 commencement address at Kenyon College], http://moreintelligentlife.com/story/david-foster-wallace-in-his-own-words [accessed February 14, 2015]).

3. Richard F. Lovelace, *Dynamics of Spiritual Life: An Evangelical Theology of Renewal* (Downers Grove, IL: InterVarsity, 1979), 101, 211–12.

4. A version of this table is found in Timothy Keller, *Gospel in Life Study Guide: Grace Changes Everything* (Grand Rapids: Zondervan, 2010), 16.

5. C. S. Lewis, *The Screwtape Letters* (New York: Macmillan, 1961), vii.

6. Paul is engaging the Stoic virtues. Fulfilling these virtues through Stoicism—a functional moralism of suppressing your emotions and denying your passions—is not sufficient. It takes being "taught" by the gospel to truly attain these virtues. Thanks to Dr. Mark Reynolds for this insight.

7. This "indicative-imperative" order and balance is everywhere in the letters of Paul. For example, Paul in the first three chapters of 1 Corinthians repeatedly reminds the Corinthian Christians that they *are* "holy"—set apart and accepted. Then in 1 Corinthians 4, 5, and 6, he tells them to "*be* what you *are*; practice your identity."

8. For considerably more on this subject, see Timothy Keller, *Counterfeit Gods* (New York: Penguin, 2009).

9. Martin Luther, *A Treatise on Good Works* (Rockville, MD: Serenity, 2009), 28.

10. Luther (*Treatise on Good Works*, 29) writes, "All those who do not at all times trust God ... but seek His favor in other things or in themselves, do not keep this Commandment, and practice real idolatry, even if they were to do the works of all the other Commandments."

11. Theologian Paul Tillich also provides helpful categories for understanding idolatry. Tillich (*Dynamics of Faith* [New York: HarperCollins, 2001]) defined faith as "ultimate concern" (p. 1). Whatever you are *living for*—whether or not you are religious—is your god. Idolatry is "the elevation of something preliminary to ultimacy" (p. 133).

12. See Timothy Keller, *Gospel in Life Study Guide* (Grand Rapids: Zondervan, 2010), for more detail on much of what is included in this chapter.

Chapter 6: The Work of Gospel Renewal

1. C. John Miller, *Outgrowing the Ingrown Church* (Grand Rapids: Zondervan, 1986, 1999), 98–101.

2. See D. Martyn Lloyd-Jones, *Revival* (Wheaton, IL: Crossway, 1987), 33–54 (chs. titled "Unbelief" and "Doctrinal Impurity").

3. See Lloyd-Jones, *Revival*, 68–79.

4. Ibid., 55–67, 80–91.

5. Bryan Chapell, *Christ-Centered Preaching: Redeeming the Expository Sermon* (2nd ed.; Grand Rapids: Baker, 2005).

6. D. Martyn Lloyd-Jones, *Spiritual Depression: Its Causes and Cure* (Grand

Rapids: Eerdmans, 1965), 23–36; Timothy Keller, *The Prodigal God: Recovering the Heart of the Christian Faith* (New York: Dutton, 2008); Timothy Keller, *The Prodigal God Discussion Guide* (Grand Rapids: Zondervan, 2009).

7. See Richard F. Lovelace, *Dynamics of Spiritual Life: An Evangelical Theology of Renewal* (Downers Grove, IL: InterVarsity, 1979, and these three books by Jonathan Edwards: *The Nature of True Virtue* (Eugene, OR: Wipf and Stock, 2003); *Thoughts on the New England Revival: Vindicating the Great Awakening* (Carlisle, PA: Banner of Truth, 2004); and *Religious Affections* (Carlisle, PA: Banner of Truth, 1961). Edwards has numerous other works on revival that are worth examining. See also his sermons "A Divine and Supernatural Light" and "Justification by Faith."

8. Helpful resources for this process include Redeemer's *Paul's Letter to the Galatians: Living in Line with the Truth of the Gospel* (facilitator guide and participant guide, http://redeemercitytocity.com/resources/library.jsp?Library_item_param=376) and Timothy Keller, *Gospel in Life Study Guide: Grace Changes Everything* (Grand Rapids: Zondervan, 2010).

9. William Williams, *The Experience Meeting: An Introduction to the Welsh Societies of the Great Awakening*, trans. D. Martyn Lloyd-Jones (Vancouver, B.C.: Regent College Publishing, 2003).

10. William B. Sprague, *Lectures on Revivals of Religion* (1832; repr., Carlisle, PA: Banner of Truth, 2007), 139.

11. Ibid., 118–29.

12. Ibid., 153–214 ("Lecture VI: Treatment Due to Awakened Sinners"; "Lecture VII: Treatment Due to Young Converts").

13. Ibid., 155.

14. The letters of John Newton, the famous hymn writer, provide another great resource for gospel counseling. A good place to start is the small paperback *The Letters of John Newton* (Carlisle, PA: Banner of Truth, 1960).

15. See Wilson H. Kimnach, "Jonathan Edwards's Pursuit of Reality," in *Jonathan Edwards and the American Experience*, ed. Nathan O. Hatch and Harry S. Stout (New York: Oxford University Press, 1988), 105.

16. D. Martyn Lloyd-Jones, "Jonathan Edwards and the Crucial Importance of Revival," in *The Puritans: Their Origins and Successors* (Edinburgh: Banner of Truth, 1976), 360.

17. This figure came from a *New York* magazine article in the early 1990s and included attendees at *all* Protestant congregations. Another study showed that the population attending *evangelical* Protestant congregations was less than 1 percent of Manhattanites at the end of the 1980s.

18. D. Martyn Lloyd-Jones, *Preaching and Preachers* (Grand Rapids: Zondervan, 1972), 151.

19. Richard F. Lovelace, *Dynamics of Spiritual Life: An Evangelical Theology of Renewal* (Downers Grove, IL: InterVarsity, 1979), 145–200.

20. Derek Kidner, *Psalms 73–150: A Commentary* (Downers Grove, IL: InterVarsity, 1973), 440.

21. Ibid.

22. Ibid.

Reflections on Gospel Renewal

1. C. S. Lewis, "Three Kinds of Men," in *Present Concerns* (London: Fount, 1986), 21–22. Tim Keller mentions this essay in the following clip: www .youtube.com/watch?v=yQOkWULpW8g (accessed February 25, 2015).

2. C. S. Lewis, "Man or Rabbit?" in *God in the Dock* (1970: repr., Grand Rapids: Eerdmans, 2002), 112.

3. Richard Lovelace, *Dynamics of Spiritual Life: An Evangelical Theology of Renewal* (Grand Rapids: Eerdmans, 1979), esp. 98–102.

4. Martin Luther, "A Sermon on the Three Kinds of Good Life for the Instruction of Consciences," in *Luther's Works*, vol. 44 (Minneapolis: Fortress, 1966), 236.

5. Ibid., 239.

6. Ibid., 240.

7. Ibid., 241–42.

8. See Clare Carlisle, *Kierkegaard: A Guide for the Perplexed* (London: Continuum, 2007), 77–83.

9. F. B. Meyer, *The Directory of the Devout Life* (London: Morgan and Scott, 1904), 148.

10. Thomas Aquinas, *Summa Theologiæ, vol. 30: The Gospel of Grace* (trans. Cornelius Ernst; Oxford: Blackfriars, 1972), 81–85.

11. Blaise Pascal, *Pensees* (Middlesex, England: Penguin, 1995), 52.

12. I haven't found a place in Edwards where he specifically speaks of three ways to live with the same clarity these others do, but he explains the moral life so frequently in terms of true versus false obedience (and thus, implicitly, three ways to live) that he deserves to be included here. To see Edwards's distinction between true and false zeal, see esp. *Religious Affections*, vol. 2 in *The Works of Jonathan Edwards*, ed. John E. Smith (New Haven, CT: Yale University Press, 1959), 163–65; idem, *The Great Awakening*, vol. 4 in *The Works of Jonathan Edwards*, ed. C. C. Goen (New Haven, CT: Yale University Press, 1972), 243, 460. We might also note Edwards's discussion of "three kinds of praise" in *The Glory and Honor of God: Volume 2 of the Previously Unpublished Sermons of Jonathan Edwards*, ed. Michael McMullen (Nashville: Broadman & Holman, 2004), 124.

13. Herman Ridderbos, *Paul: An Outline of His Theology*, trans. John Richard de Witt (Grand Rapids: Eerdmans, 1975), 137–40.

14. Karl Barth, *Church Dogmatics*, ed. G. W. Bromiley and T. F. Torrance (Edinburgh: T&T Clark, 1961), IV/3, 461–62.

15. See Dane C. Ortlund, "Christocentrism: An Asymmetrical Trinitarianism?" *Themelios* 34 (2009): 309–21.

16. J. Gresham Machen, *What Is Faith?* (1925; repr., Edinburgh: Banner of Truth, 1991), 173.

17. Richard Lovelace, whom Keller quotes regarding the relationship of sanctification to justification (pp. 116–17), returns repeatedly to the truth of union with Christ in *Dynamics of Spiritual Life* (e.g., pp. 73–81, 98, 103–4, 114–15, 133, 142, 145, 170, 189, 194).

18. John Calvin, *Institutes of the Christian Religion*, ed. John T. McNeill (Philadelphia: Westminster, 1960), 1:537.

19. Charles Hodge, *The Way of Life: A Handbook of Christian Belief and Practice* (1841; repr., Grand Rapids: Baker, 1977), 325.

20. Though much has been written on this doctrine in recent years, the definitive book on Paul's theology of union with Christ is now Constantine R. Campbell, *Paul and Union with Christ: An Exegetical and Theological Study* (Grand Rapids: Zondervan, 2012). Campbell identifies four senses to Paul's use of union with Christ: union, participation, identification, and incorporation.

21. Greg Beale explores the ways inaugurated eschatology fuels Christian living in the final chapter of *A New Testament Biblical Theology: The Unfolding of the Old Testament in the New* (Grand Rapids: Baker, 2011), 835–70, 961–62.

22. A useful dialogue partner here is Donald L. Alexander, ed., *Christian Spirituality: Five Views of Sanctification* (Downers Grove, IL: InterVarsity, 1989). Sinclair Ferguson outlines the Reformed view of sanctification with which Tim Keller confessionally aligns, yet the chapters on gospel renewal at times sound more like Gerhard Forde's outline of the Lutheran view. The key difference Ferguson draws out as distinguishing his view from Lutheranism is the paradigmatic significance of union with Christ (e.g., pp. 34, 51). Similarly Sinclair Ferguson, *John Owen on the Christian Life* (Edinburgh: Banner of Truth, 1987), 130.

23. In the DMin course at Reformed Theological Seminary he co-taught for several years with Edmund Clowney, Keller draws on the work of the Dutch Reformed theologian G. C. Berkouwer to argue that justification fuels sanctification. One sees this emphasis in Keller's gospel renewal chapters too, and it is a profound insight that is clearly biblical. Yet Berkouwer himself failed to sufficiently integrate union with Christ with his soteriology more broadly (as I argue in Dane C. Ortlund, "Sanctification by Justification: The Forgotten Insight of Bavinck and Berkouwer on Progressive Sanctification," *Scottish Bulletin of Evangelical Theology* 28 [2010]: 43–61). Our evangelical forebearer Carl Henry criticized Berkouwer at this very point (Carl F. H. Henry, *Christian Personal Ethics* [Grand Rapids: Eerdmans, 1957], 468–71).

24. Humphrey Carpenter, ed., *The Letters of J. R. R. Tolkien* (New York: Houghton Mifflin, 2000), 110.

25. I owe this latter articulation to Jared Wilson.

26. I am grateful to my dad, Ray Ortlund, for pointing out to me this insight of Spurgeon's.

27. As Thomas Watson points out in *A Body of Divinity* (London: Banner of Truth, 1965), 187.

28. John Owen, *Communion with the Triune God*, ed. Kelly M. Kapic and Justin Taylor (Wheaton, IL: Crossway, 2007), 251.

29. Thomas Goodwin, *The Heart of Christ* (Edinburgh: Banner of Truth, 2011), 48. Goodwin's full title was *The Heart of Christ in Heaven Towards Sinners on Earth; Or, A Treatise Demonstrating the Gracious Disposition and Tender Affection of Christ in his Human Nature Now in Glory, Unto His Members under All Sorts of Infirmities, Either of Sin or Misery.* Other Puritans similarly focus on the heart of God: e.g., Thomas Manton, *Exposition of John 17* (London: Banner of Truth, 1959); William Bridge, *A Lifting Up for the Downcast* (Edinburgh: Banner of Truth, 1961); Thomas Brooks, *Precious Remedies Against Satan's Devices* (London: Banner of Truth, 1968); John Bunyan, *Come and Welcome to Jesus Christ* (Edinburgh: Banner of Truth, 2004).

30. Bryan Chapell, *Holiness by Grace: Delighting in the Joy That Is Our Strength* (Wheaton, IL: Crossway, 2001), 196. I have been asked to interact specifically with Tim Keller's content in *Center Church*, but I must add that when his entire preaching ministry is in view, one does find the nuance I am describing here.

31. I am grateful to Drew Hunter, Scott Kauffmann, and Gavin Ortlund for their careful reading of and response to an early draft of this chapter.

Response to Dane Ortlund

1. John Calvin, *Institutes of the Christian Religion*, ed. John T. McNeill (Philadelphia: Westminster, 1960), 1:48.

2. Douglas Moo, *The Epistle to the Romans* (New International Commentary on the New Testament; Grand Rapids: Eerdmans, 1996), 351–52.

3. John Owen, *Of the Mortification of Sin in Believers*, www.ccel.org/ccel/owen/mort (accessed August 31, 2015).

ABOUT THE
CONTRIBUTORS

Michael Horton (PhD, University of Coventry and Wycliffe Hall, Oxford) is the J. Gresham Machen Professor of Systematic Theology and Apologetics at Westminster Seminary California. He is the president of White Horse Media, for which he co-hosts the White Horse Inn, a nationally syndicated, weekly radio talk show exploring issues of Reformation theology in American Christianity. The editor in chief of *Modern Reformation* magazine, Horton is the author of more than twenty publications.

Dane Ortlund (PhD, Wheaton College) is executive vice president and Bible publisher at Crossway in Wheaton, Illinois, where he lives with his wife and their five children. He is the author of several books and co-editor of *Short Studies in Biblical Theology* and *Knowing the Bible* and has written numerous articles in both scholarly and popular venues.

Loving the City

Doing Balanced, Gospel-Centered Ministry in Your City

Timothy Keller, with new contributions by Daniel Strange, Gabriel Salguero, and Andy Crouch

In *Loving the City*, bestselling author and pastor Timothy Keller looks at the biblical foundations for contextualizing the gospel as we communicate to the culture in a way that is both respectful and challenging. He articulates the key characteristics of a city vision, showing how the city develops as a theme throughout Scripture, from its anti-God origins to its strategic importance for mission to its culmination and redemption in glory.

    Loving the City contains the second section of *Center Church* in an easy-to-read format with new essays from several other contributors and Tim Keller's responses to the essays.

Serving a Movement

Doing Balanced, Gospel-Centered Ministry in Your City

Timothy Keller, with new contributions by Tim Chester, Daniel Montgomery and Mike Cosper, and Alan Hirsch

In *Serving a Movement*, bestselling author and pastor Timothy Keller looks at the nature of the church's mission and its relationship to the work of individual Christians in the world. He examines what it means to be a "missional" church today and how churches can practically equip people for missional living. Churches need to intentionally cultivate an integrative ministry that connects people to God, to one another, to the needs of the city, and to the culture around us. Finally, he highlights the need for intentional movements of churches planting new churches that faithfully proclaim God's truth and serve their communities.

    Serving a Movement contains the third section of *Center Church* in an easy-to-read format with new essays from several other contributors and Tim Keller's responses to the essays.

" Because the world is on its way to becoming 75 percent urban, we all need a theological vision that is distinctly urban. Even if you don't go to the city. . . make no mistake, the city is coming to you. "

—Tim Keller, *Center Church*

Redeemer City to City finds and develops leaders in the art and science of starting new churches.

After fifteen years of coaching and training urban church planters, we are making our training available to the public for the first time.

+ New in-depth training in gospel-centered ministry

+ Courses on Center Church, Gospel Renewal, and Ministry Design

+ New and original video teaching by Tim Keller, CTC staff, and church planters

redeemercitytocity.com/learning

REDEEMER CITY to CITY

Any reader of *Center Church* might be interested to know that Timothy Keller founded an organization called Redeemer City to City.

Redeemer City to City carries out the ministry principles you've read about in this book around the world. Coaching and training urban church planters and starting gospel movements in global cities are at the core of CTC's mission.

If you'd like to know more about Redeemer City to City's work, write to us at hello@redeemercitytocity.com.

May Jesus Christ be known in cities.